7-18

Flipping Out with Debra Murray

The Ultimate Flip Pan Cookbook

Flipping Out with Debra Murray
ISBN 978-1-4951-6532-0

Printed in the U.S.A.

I dedicate this book in memory of

Sherri Campbell

You touched the lives of all who knew you.
It melted me to know how much you
loved your Jumbo Flip pan!

I am so thrilled with the success of our Cook's Companion Flip Pans! Curtis Anderson—you are a genius!

Thank you Mark Linduski for helping Curt design and for all your wonderful support over the past two years. You are an angel to me!

I must thank my beautiful daughter Nevar; you are not only beautiful, but smart and fun! You are my best friend! Thanks for always encouraging me! I have the best mom, dad, sister, and bonus mom, Myrna. Thanks for all your love and support!

I am so grateful for our Fabulous group on Facebook, The Flip Pan Group. To date we have over 3,000 members and growing. It delights me daily to see your posts and how you all constantly encourage each other. I could not keep up if it were not for my dear friend Josephine Cook (below, left). Michael Caldwell, thank you for always making all of us smile. I adore all my friends on Facebook—you make me feel so loved, and your encouragement and support of my shows means the world to me. I have one special viewer who melts my heart. It's young Jarod (center). He had his mom Beth buy a juicer I was demonstrating, and he took the juicer to school to encourage his classmates to juice for better health. I adore that young man. He is currently 12, and has been accepted into the culinary program from middle school. So proud that I have inspired him to cook and teach his peers!

A special thanks to Chef Daniel Green for contributing his delicious Party Burger recipe. It is an honor and joy to work with you, my friend.

I want to thank Rick Campbell for allowing us to shoot in his gorgeous condo! Chris Davis— my brilliant and ever-so-talented photographer—thank you for your magic. Thanks to Diane Linder for editing this book and Erin White for styling my live shows. But most of all I would like to thank my best friend, Laurie Bain (pictured with Chris). I could not have done it without you, my friend! She typed, tested, food-styled, and has just been there for me like no one else . . . love you buddy!

Contents

Tips for Success with Flip Pans

The Flip Pan, when closed by the magnet, is two pans attached with a gasket, that will retain 90 percent of the cooking steam, turning the pan into a low-pressure pressure cooker. This means you will retain more flavor and more nutrients than cooking with other pans. You will also experience faster cooking times. In this book I have included more than a hundered recipes, some for the Jumbo Flip Pan and some for the Original Flip Pan. Plus, we would like to welcome to our family the Round Flip Pan, and our newest star, The Triple Flip.

Low pressure cooking is done at approximately 3 PSI. While the liquid or moisture from cooking food creates steam, prohibiting the escape of the steam reduces cooking time compared to using a conventional covered pot—water boils at a higher temperature under pressure, thus speeding up the cooking process. Additionally, bathing food in steam seals in flavor and nutrients that are typically boiled out on the stovetop. So with the Flip Pans, you get better tasting, juicier meals faster!

The first thing I always recommend (and the manufacturer, too) is to clean your Flip Pan with soap and water, towel dry, then rub the ceramic surface with olive oil to season it. The ceramic is a fabulous water-based, chemical-free nonstick coating. Like any water-based product, occasionally seasoning the surface will give it longer life. To have optimum release, I recommend using a nonstick spray. There are tremendous new pump, non-aerosol, nonstick spray products in the grocery stores that are healthy—like grapeseed and coconut. Most of my recipes will call for preheating without oil or spray, top and bottom. But I am a person who will never leave a pan unattended. If you find you may leave the pan in the preheat stage, I recommend adding oil to the pan so the nonstick surface does not turn brown. I heat my pan until I feel the heat coming off the pan, then I add the spray or oil.

I know we call the Flip Pan a flip pan—but that does not mean everything needs to be flipped. Some recipes call for adding cooking liquid, and because of the steam hole, this will create a mess on your stove if you were to flip it. For other recipes, the added weight of the food could cause the pan to open while turning.

My favorite technique is to brown the protein on both sides (flipping when using the Original) then add my liquids, such as stock or wine. For the Jumbo Flip Pan, I flip only when making popcorn—and even then—only kettle Corn.

For best results cooking proteins: The first thing I do when cooking any protein is to make sure the poultry, steak, pork, fish or seafood is very dry—all residual moisture removed. I let my proteins sit at room temperature for at least 20 minutes. Then, I rub with just enough oil to adhere the seasonings I will be putting on them. Next, I make sure the pan is hot. I love to begin with a 2-minute sear per side on medium-high, then I reduce the temperature to medium. Typically I keep the flip pan closed for nearly all dishes, except steak, tuna or scallops. For steak, tuna, and scallops, I will cook the recipe 90 percent of the way through before closing the lid for the last minute or two to infuse the protein with its cooking liquid. For other meats, I like to preheat the Flip Pan's top and bottom, then cook about 5 minutes per side for a chicken breast, for example.

How to calculate meat cooking times: This is not an exact science, but I have found that if I preheat the pan top and bottom, and because of the low pressure the pan creates while closed, I take all typical cook times and cut them in half. If a recipe calls for pork chops to cook 10 minutes per side for ½-inch thick chops, I cook them for 5 minutes per side. Every now and again, I wish I had cooked them a bit less, or I needed to give them a few minutes longer. But ninety percent of the time that is the perfect calculation.

I give you these recipes as a template—feel free to add more spices or different ingredients. Make them your own. I usually give you a timeframe that will not allow the recipe to overcook, but when you open the lid, check to make sure it is cooked to your liking. But remember, there can be variations where, say, the chicken may need a few minutes longer.

I am so happy you have purchased our fabulous pans, and I hope you have as much joy using them that I and all my wonderful friends in the Flip Pan Group on Facebook have experienced, including some of the most loyal recipe posters who contributed Flip Pan recipes to this newest collection. Be prepared to be flipped out over all the things you can do with these incredible pans. Happy Cooking!!

Love,
Debra Murray

Cooking Chart for Flip Pans

Here is a basic cooking guideline for proteins, vegetables, pasta and rice. I did not include sandwiches, since these would depend on thickness and ingredients. There are sandwich recipes in this book you can use as a guideline.

When reading the chart, under Cooking Time note that PS means *per side*. If you are using the Original, Round or Triple Flip Pan, you would flip the pan; when using the jumbo Flip Pan you open the pan and flip the food, then re-seal.

FOOD	THICKNESS/ WEIGHT	COOKING TEMPERATURE	COOKING TIME	LIQUID NEEDED	READY WHEN
PROTEINS					
Bacon	6 Strips	Medium	3 Minutes PS	No	Medium
Barbecued Ribs	½ Slab	Medium-High	15 Minutes PS	Yes	Well
Burgers	1–1½ Inches Thick	Medium-High	4–5 Minutes PS	No	Med/Well
Chicken	1–1½ Inches Thick	Medium-High	5 Minutes PS	Choose	Well
Chicken Thighs	1 Pound	Medium-High	8 Minutes PS	Choose	Well
Corned Beef	3 Pounds	Medium	4 Hours	Yes	Well
Drumsticks	1 Pound	Medium-High	7 Minutes PS	Choose	Well
Eggs	2 Large	Medium	2 Minutes PS	No	Runny
Fish Filets	1 Pound	Medium-High	2 Minutes PS	Yes	Well
Ham Steak	1 Inch Thick	Medium-High	3 Minutes PS	No	Well
Pork Chops	1–1½ Inches Thick	Medium	10 Minutes PS	Yes	Well
Pork Roast	3 Pounds	Medium	2½ Hours	Yes	Well
Pot Roast	3 Pounds	Medium	3 Hours	Yes	Well
Salmon	1 Pound	Medium-High	3 Minutes	No	Well
Sausages	1 Pound	Medium-High	5 Minutes PS	Yes	Well
Shrimp	1 Pound	Medium	3 Minutes PS	Choose	Med/Well
Spare Ribs	6 Ribs	Medium-High	20 Minutes PS	Yes	Well
Spatchcock	3 Pounds	Medium-High	12 Minutes PS	Choose	Well
Steak	1–1½ Inches Thick	Medium-High	3–4 Minutes PS	No	Medium Rare

FOOD	THICKNESS/ WEIGHT	COOKING TEMPERATURE	COOKING TIME	LIQUID NEEDED	READY WHEN
VEGETABLES					
Artichokes	2 Halves	Medium-High	10 Minutes PS	Yes	Tender
Asparagus	1 Pound	Medium-High	2 Minutes PS	Yes	Tender
Broccoli	1 Pound	Medium-High	4 Minutes	Yes	Tender
Brussels Sprouts	1 Pound	Medium-High	10 Minutes	Yes	Tender
Carrots	6–7 Medium	Medium-High	7 Minutes	Yes	Tender
Corn	4 Ears	Medium-High	4 Minutes PS	Yes	Tender
Eggplant	1 Medium	Medium-High	5 Minutes PS	No	Tender
Green Beans	1 Pound	Medium-High	9 Minutes	Yes	Tender
Kale	1 Pound	Medium-High	8 Minutes	Yes	Tender
Mushrooms	1 Pound	Medium-High	4 Minutes PS	Yes	Tender
Onions	1 Pound	Medium-High	4 Minutes PS	No	Tender
Peppers	2 Medium	Medium-High	3 Minutes PS	No	Tender
Potatoes	2 Pounds	Medium-High	20 Minutes	Yes	Tender
Winter Squash	2 Pounds	Medium-High	12 Minutes	Yes	Tender
Zucchini	1 Pound	Medium-High	3 Minutes PS	No	Tender
GRAINS					
Pasta	2 Cups Dry 4 Cups in Boiling Liquid	Medium-High	8–10 Minutes	Yes	Al Dente
Quinoa	2 Cups Dry 2 Cups in Boiling Liquid	Medium	12 Minutes	Yes	Fluffy
Rice, White	2 Cups Dry 3 Cups in Boiling Liquid	Medium	15 Minutes	Yes	Fluffy

Recipes for Your Flip Pan

Original Flip Pan
12–47

Jumbo Flip Pan
94–129

Round Flip Pan
48–91

Triple Flip Pan
130–162

Original Flip Pan

Baha Fat-Free Turkey Burgers

Servings: 4

INGREDIENTS

1 envelope fajita seasoning
10 button mushrooms
¼ cup water
1 pound ground turkey breast
4 large lettuce leaves
salsa

DIRECTIONS

In a food processor, combine seasoning, mushrooms, and water; transfer to a bowl and let rest for 10 minutes.

Add turkey to the bowl; mix well and form 4 equal sized patties.

Preheat Flip Pan 2 minutes per side over medium heat.

Place burgers in Flip Pan; close lid.

Cook for 5 minutes per side.

Serve burgers wrapped in lettuce leaves and top with fresh salsa.

Cherie Bream Estok's Liver and Onions

Servings: 2

Cherie is one of my favorites from the Flip Pan Group.
She is always nurturing and encouraging others.

INGREDIENTS

1 tablespoon oil, plus small amount for heating pan

¼ cup of all-purpose flour

1 pound of beef liver, sliced

pinch of salt and pepper (to taste)

1 large onion (sliced)

DIRECTIONS

Heat the pan over medium heat, approximately 3 minutes per side, with a small amount of oil.

While the pan is heating, put the flour, salt and pepper into a plastic bag and add the beef liver and shake thoroughly to coat the liver.

Add the tablespoon of oil to the hot pan and place the flour-dredged liver into the oil.

Close the lid and cook for approximately three minutes. Flip and cook for another three minutes.

Add the onion slices and cook for another three to four minutes, flipping the pan during the cooking process.

Grilled Polenta

Servings: 2

INGREDIENTS

1 cup water
1 cup yellow corn meal
nonstick cooking spray
½ teaspoon sea salt

DIRECTIONS

Pour water with salt into a saucepan and bring to a boil.

Add cornmeal to saucepan; whisk well.

Lower the heat and cook for 8 minutes while stirring constantly.

Apply nonstick spray to 9-inch baking pan and spread the cornmeal into the pan; cover and chill for 8 hours.

Preheat Flip Pan, top and bottom, on medium heat for 2–3 minutes per side.

Cut polenta into desired shapes.

Place polenta into Flip Pan; close lid.

Cook for 5 minutes per side, serve immediately.

Grilled Peaches and Raspberry Sorbet

Servings: 2

INGREDIENTS

2 firm peaches, halved, pits removed
¼ cup Chambord raspberry liqueur
½ teaspoon fresh lemon juice
1 teaspoon sugar, divided
butter-flavored nonstick cooking spray
raspberry sorbet

DIRECTIONS

In a bowl, combine peaches, liqueur, and lemon juice; let marinate for 30 minutes.

Preheat Flip Pan, top and bottom, on medium heat for 2–3 minutes per side.

Fill the hole of each peach half with sugar.

Apply nonstick to Flip Pan.

Place peaches, skin side down, in Flip Pan; close lid.

Cook for 3 minutes per side and serve hot or cold with raspberry sorbet.

Grilled Lamb Chops

Servings: 2–4

INGREDIENTS

1 rack of lamb, cut into individual chops and trimmed of fat
1 cup Balsamic Marinade, divided, page 163
2 sprigs rosemary
8 Roma tomatoes, halved
¼ cup My Favorite Pesto, page 166

DIRECTIONS

In a bowl, combine ¼ cup marinade and lamb chops; let marinate in the refrigerator for 1 hour.

Preheat Flip Pan, top and bottom, on medium heat for 2–3 minutes per side.

Place lamb chops and rosemary in Flip Pan; cook for 2 minutes with lid open, turn and cook for 2 minutes longer. Close the Flip Pan and cook for 3 minutes longer for medium rare, transfer to a platter.

Dip tomatoes into reserved ¼ cup marinade and place them flesh side down in the Flip Pan; close lid.

Cook for 2 minutes per side.

Top tomatoes with pesto and serve them with the lamb chops.

Grilled Asparagus

Servings: 2

INGREDIENTS

- 1 pound asparagus, washed, trimmed and peeled
- 1 tablespoon extra-virgin olive oil
- ½ tablespoon fresh lemon juice
- ½ teaspoon sea salt
- ¼ teaspoon fresh ground pepper
- 1 teaspoon fresh chopped mint leaves

DIRECTIONS

Place all ingredients in a one-gallon zipper bag and let marinate for 30 minutes.

Preheat Flip Pan, top and bottom, on medium heat for 2–3 minutes per side.

Place all the asparagus in Flip Pan; do not stack; close lid.

Cook for 3 minutes per side and serve.

Torchia Homan's
Easy Stove Top Pan Pizza

Servings: 4

INGREDIENTS

½ cup self-rising flour

½ cup all-purpose flour

⅔ cup lukewarm water

pinch of salt

1 rounded teaspoon dry yeast

1 teaspoon honey

pizza sauce

favorite toppings

mozzarella cheese

DIRECTIONS

Gently combine first 6 ingredients in your Flip Pan with a whisk.

With your fingers, press in pan until bottom is covered.

Cover with your favorite pizza sauce.

Add your favorite toppings.

Top with mozzarella cheese.

Cook on medium heat for 15 minutes with the lid closed.

Then cook for 5 minutes with the lid open. (Until desired crispness of crust)

Ratatouille

Servings: 4

Delicious over pasta, or as a side dish or even in an omelet.
This recipe works in the original Flip Pan or the round Flip Pan.

INGREDIENTS

2 tablespoons extra virgin olive oil

1 medium sweet onion, sliced thin

2 bell peppers, julienned

2 cloves garlic, minced

1 medium eggplant, peeled and diced

1 medium zucchini, cut into ½-inch slices

1 medium crookneck squash, cut into ½-inch slices

½ teaspoon sea salt

½ teaspoon fresh ground pepper

1 14.5-ounce can petite diced tomatoes

1 sprig thyme

DIRECTIONS

Preheat the Flip Pan top and bottom over medium heat for several minutes per side.

Add the oil and heat for 2 minutes.

Add the onions and peppers and close lid and cook for 2 minutes.

Open and add the garlic and close and cook for 1 minute longer.

Add the eggplant, squashes, and salt and pepper.

Cook for 2 minutes then flip. Cook for 3 minutes then flip back.

Stir in the tomatoes and add the thyme sprig. Cook covered over medium heat
    5 minutes longer.

Marian Minicozzi's Stuffed Chicken Breast with Zucchini Spaghetti

Servings: 4

INGREDIENTS

4 boneless, skinless chicken breasts

6 tablespoons sweet chili sauce, divided

½ cup goat cheese

4mini peppers

½ cup grated mozzarella cheese (full or part-skim)

2 egg whites

½ cup panko bread crumbs

2 teaspoons extra-virgin olive oil

1 tablespoon of sweet chili sauce

1 large zucchini, cut into noodle strips by hand; use a vegetti or any spiral slicer or peeler

DIRECTIONS

Cut a horizontal slit along the long edge of a chicken breast, nearly through to the opposite side. Repeat with all the chicken breasts.

Add 4 tablespoons of the sweet chili sauce to a bowl with the chicken so it can marinate while you make the stuffing for the peppers. Mix well.

Mix the goat cheese and 2 tablespoons of the sweet chili sauce in a small bowl.

Cut mini peppers in half lengthwise so they can be stuffed with goat cheese mixture.

Spread open each chicken breast and place 2 of the stuffed peppers in a line, but not on top of one another.

Then sprinkle grated mozzarella on top of mini peppers.

Close the breast over the filling, pressing the edges firmly together to seal. Repeat with the remaining chicken breasts and filling. Secure with a toothpick or skewer.

Lightly beat egg white with a fork in a medium bowl. Place breadcrumbs in a shallow dish.

Dip each chicken breast in the egg white; then dredge in breadcrumbs.

Preheat Flip Pan on medium-high for 2 minutes per side. Open Flip Pan and add the oil; let heat for 1 minute longer.

Add chicken breasts; cook with lid closed until browned on one side, about 5 minutes. Flip the pan with the lid closed. Open the Flip Pan and add some sweet chili sauce on top of cooked chicken. Close and continue to cook for another 5 minutes or until the chicken is no longer pink in the center or until an instant-read thermometer registers 170°F.

Add more chili sauce on top before serving, if desired.

Remove the chicken breasts to a platter and add the zucchini noodles to the Flip Pan with additional sauce. Close and cook for three minutes.

Open the Flip Pan and take out zucchini noodles and serve with stuffed chicken cutlets.

Patty Torchia Homan's Mini Meatloaves

Servings: 6

INGREDIENTS

1 pound ground beef

¾ cup bread crumbs

1 egg

¼ cup finely chopped onion

1 teaspoon finely chopped garlic

¼ teaspoon salt

¼ teaspoon coarse ground pepper

1 teaspoon parsley flakes

1 teaspoon celery flakes

¼ cup catsup

4–5 medium Yukon potatoes (quartered)

2 cups baby carrots

2 packs of gravy mixes

DIRECTIONS

Combine in bowl the ground beef, bread crumbs, egg, onion, and garlic.

Add salt, pepper, parsley flakes, celery flakes, and catsup.

Mix well, divide into six portions, and shape into mini meatloaves.

Arrange in your Flip Pan along with the potatoes and baby carrots.

Prepare the gravy mix as directed and pour over meatloaf, potatoes, and carrots.

With Flip Pan lid closed, cook over medium heat for 30 minutes; turn over meatloaves and continue cooking for 15 minutes until done.

Grilled Summer Squash

Servings: 4

✳ This recipe can be done in all the Flip Pans. For the Jumbo Flip Pan, you would just cook with the lid on and turn the squash with tongs.

INGREDIENTS

2 medium zucchini
2 medium crookneck squash
1 tablespoon olive oil
1 teaspoon fresh thyme leaves
½ teaspoon sea salt
¼ teaspoon freshly ground pepper
juice from 1 lemon

DIRECTIONS

Slice the zucchini lengthwise and then chop crosswise, creating half-moon slices.

Repeat with the crookneck squash.

Place the squash in a bowl and toss with remaining ingredients.

Preheat Flip Pan top and bottom over medium heat several minutes per side.

With grill side down, add the squash slices to the Flip Pan.

Increase the heat to medium-high and cook for 3 minutes, then flip and cook for 3 minutes on the other side.

Macaroni and Cheese

Servings: 4

INGREDIENTS

2 cups chicken stock

2½ cups dry elbow macaroni

1 cup heavy cream

1 tablespoon whipped cream cheese

1½ cup cheddar cheese, shredded

1½ cup mozzarella cheese, shredded

½ cup Parmesan cheese

DIRECTIONS

Place Flip Pan on stove and add the chicken stock. Bring to a boil.

When stock comes to a boil, add the dry pasta, close lid and set timer for 8 minutes.

When cook time is complete, add the cream and cheeses, stirring until smooth.

Cook over low until smooth and creamy.

Serve immediately.

Jerri Kendall Hegarty Cook's Chicken Lazone

Servings: 4

You can make this in the round Flip Pan as well.

INGREDIENTS

½ teaspoon salt
1½ teaspoons chili powder
1½ teaspoons onion powder
2 teaspoons garlic powder
¼ teaspoon cayenne pepper
2 lbs. chicken tenders
¼ cup butter divided
2 cups heavy cream

DIRECTIONS

Combine the first five ingredients in a bowl.

Toss the chicken tenders into the spice mixture.

Preheat Flip Pan top and bottom over medium heat for 2–3 minutes per side.

Add half of the butter to the Flip Pan and increase the heat to medium-high.

Add the chicken tenders and cook for 4–5 minutes, then flip and continue cooking 4 minutes longer.

Flip again, and then add the cream and the remaining butter.

Cook with Flip Pan open to reduce the cream while scraping up the bits from the bottom of the pan. Cook for approximately 5 minutes.

Serve with pasta or mashed potatoes.

Georgina Budney's Eggplant Rollitini

Servings: 4

   * *This recipe can be made in the Original Flip Pan and the Round Flip Pan.*

INGREDIENTS

1 medium eggplant

salt

15 ounces ricotta cheese

1 large egg

8 ounces mozzarella cheese, divided

¼ teaspoon red pepper flakes

¼ teaspoon garlic powder

2 cups of fresh spinach

1 jar of red sauce

DIRECTIONS

Cut eggplant lengthwise in ⅛-inch slices. Salt each side and set aside.

Mix ricotta, egg, half of mozzarella, red pepper flakes, garlic powder, and chopped spinach in bowl.

Heat small Flip Pan on each side on medium heat. Open lid on grill side. Pour enough red sauce to cover the bottom of pan. Take a tablespoon of mixture, place at one end of eggplant and roll. Place seam down in pan.

Spoon 1 cup of red sauce on top lightly. Close lid and reduce to low. Cook for 20 minutes.

Open lid and sprinkle remaining mozzarella on top. Close lid for 5 minutes and open.

Barbara Williams'
Polish Noodles and Cabbage

Servings: 4

INGREDIENTS

1 16-ounce package egg noodles

½ pound bacon

2 medium onions, chopped

2 tablespoons butter

1 head of cabbage, thinly sliced

1 cup sour cream

DIRECTIONS

Cook noodles according to package directions.

Cook bacon in large Flip Pan until crispy and remove from pan and set aside.

Add chopped onions to pan and caramelize in bacon drippings.

When onions are golden brown, add the butter.

Add sliced cabbage to butter and onions and cook until tender.

Add noodles to pan and mix all together.

Crumble bacon and add to pan and mix well.

Add sour cream and serve.

Sharon Huskey's
Cheese Steak Sandwiches

Servings: 4

INGREDIENTS

¼ cup low sodium soy sauce

½ lemon, juiced

½ teaspoon garlic powder

¼ teaspoon smoked paprika

¼ teaspoon black pepper

1 pound boneless ribeye, sliced ¼-inch thick
(butcher will cut at your request)

1 tablespoon mayonnaise

4 hoagie rolls

½ sliced bell pepper

½ sliced onion

1 cup shredded six-cheese, Italian

DIRECTIONS

To prepare marinade, place soy sauce, lemon juice, garlic powder, paprika and black pepper into a one-gallon slide lock bag.

Place the steak in the bag and marinade for 1 hour.

Spread mayonnaise on the inside of the rolls.

Preheat Flip Pan top and bottom for 2 minutes per side over medium heat.

Toast the rolls in the Flip Pan 2–3 minutes each, mayonnaise side down. Set aside.

Place steak in Flip Pan on grill side and cook 2½ minutes. Flip & cook another 2 minutes. Flip again. Check meat for doneness to your taste.

Move the meat to one end of the pan & toss in onions and peppers. Close lid and cook 3½ minutes. (I like 1 to keep a little texture in them).

Stir meat, onions, & peppers evenly.

Spread cheese over meat and vegetables. Close the lid and remove from heat. Allow cheese to melt for several minutes.

Serve on grilled buns.

Spatchcock Cornish Game Hens

Servings: 2

INGREDIENTS

2 Cornish game hens, butterflied

1 cup Mojo Marinade, page 164

nonstick cooking spray

1 medium onion, quartered

1 red bell pepper, cut into 1-inch pieces

DIRECTIONS

Place Cornish hens and marinade into a one-gallon zipper bag; let marinate for 2 hours.

Preheat Flip Pan, top and bottom, on medium heat for 2–3 minutes per side.

Apply nonstick spray to Flip Pan.

Place game hens, skin side down, in Flip Pan, add the onion and pepper; close lid.

Cook for 12 minutes per side or until cooked through.

Serve over rice.

Peach Napoleons

Servings: 2

INGREDIENTS

1 cup canola oil
1 teaspoon sugar
¼ teaspoon ground cinnamon
6 wonton skins
½ cup lemon pudding
½ cup whipped topping
nonstick cooking spray
2 peaches, cut into thin wedges
powdered sugar

DIRECTIONS

Heat oil in Flip Pan until temperature reaches 350 degrees.

In a bowl, combine sugar and cinnamon.

Fry wonton skins for 1 minute on each side or until lightly browned.

Place wonton skins on paper towels to drain excess oil.

Sprinkle cinnamon mixture over wontons.

In a separate bowl, combine pudding and whipped topping; fold gently.

Remove the oil from Flip Pan and wipe.

Preheat Flip Pan, top and bottom, on medium heat for 2–3 minutes per side.

Apply nonstick spray to Flip Pan.

Place peaches in Flip Pan; close lid.

Cook for 2 minutes per side.

Ladle 1 tablespoon pudding mixture in the center of each plate.

Top 1 wonton with 1 scoop of pudding and 4 peach slices; finish the top with 1 wonton.

Place Napoleon towers on prepared plates. Dust with powdered sugar.

Peanut Butter and Banana Panini

Servings: 1–2

INGREDIENTS

2 slices English muffin bread

½ teaspoon butter, softened

1 tablespoon crunchy peanut butter

1 small banana, sliced

1 tablespoon marshmallow cream spread

DIRECTIONS

Spread butter on one side of each bread slice and place them butter-side down on a cutting board.

Top one bread slice with peanut butter and bananas.

Spread marshmallow cream on the other bread slice.

Combine both sides to make a sandwich.

Preheat Flip Pan, top and bottom, on medium heat for 2–3 minutes per side.

Place sandwich in Flip Pan; close lid.

Cook for 2 minutes per side and serve.

Pigs in a Blanket

Servings: 4

INGREDIENTS

4 jumbo hot dogs, spit horizontally
¼ cup cheddar cheese, shredded
4 slices bacon

DIRECTIONS

Fill one hotdog with cheese and wrap it in a slice of bacon; secure with a toothpick.

Repeat with remaining ingredients.

Preheat Flip Pan, top and bottom, on medium heat for 2–3 minutes per side.

Place hot dogs in Flip Pan; close lid.

Cook for 3 minutes; open Flip Pan, turn dogs with tongs, and close and cook
for 3–4 minutes longer.

Perfect Patty Melt

Servings: 2

INGREDIENTS

2 teaspoons extra-virgin olive oil

1 small onion, cut into ¼-inch slices

1 teaspoon salt

1 pound ground chuck

4 slices rye or pumpernickel bread

2 tablespoons Thousand Island dressing

4 slices cheddar cheese

DIRECTIONS

Drizzle oil over onions slices and season with salt.

Place onion slices in Flip Pan; close lid.

Cook for 3 minutes per side; remove to a plate.

Form the chuck into two equal size patties.

Preheat Flip Pan, top and bottom, on medium heat for 2–3 minutes per side.

Place patties in Flip Pan; close lid.

Cook for 6 minutes per side or until desired doneness.

Transfer patties to a platter and wipe excess fat from Flip Pan.

Place each patty on 1 bread slice.

Top each patty with dressing, half of the grilled onions and 2 slices of cheese. Cover with other bread slice.

Cook for 2 minutes per side and serve.

Philly Cheesesteak

Servings: 2

INGREDIENTS

1 tablespoon extra-virgin olive oil

1 medium onion, thinly sliced

1 red bell pepper, thinly sliced

1 pound rib eye or sirloin steak, shaved

½ teaspoon sea salt

pinch of freshly ground pepper

1 tablespoon mayonnaise

2 Italian rolls, sliced lengthwise

2 slices American cheese

1 slice provolone cheese

DIRECTIONS

Preheat Flip Pan, top and bottom, on medium heat for 2–3 minutes per side.

Pour oil in the Flip Pan and let heat for 2 minutes.

Place onions, peppers, and steak in Flip Pan; season with salt and pepper.

Close lid and cook for 2 minutes, open lid and cook for additional 3 minutes while pulling apart the meat with silicone spatulas.

Remove steak and onions to a platter.

Spread mayonnaise on the inside of each roll and place mayonnaise-side down on griddle side of Flip Pan; grill for 3 minutes, lid open.

Place steak mixture on the roll and top with cheese.

Place sandwich back in Flip Pan; close lid.

Cook for 2 minutes or until cheese is melted.

Serve immediately.

Portobello Flatbread

Servings: 2

INGREDIENTS

2 portobello mushrooms, cleaned and sliced into ½-inch pieces
1 shallot, minced
½ cup Balsamic Marinade, page 163
4 ounces goat cheese
1 flatbread, 8 inches in size
4 ounces mozzarella cheese, shredded
nonstick cooking spray

DIRECTIONS

In a bowl, combine mushrooms, shallots, and marinade; let marinate for 1 hour.

Drain mushrooms and shallots; set aside.

Preheat Flip Pan, top and bottom, on medium heat for 2–3 minutes per side.

Add the mushrooms to the Flip Pan and cook for 3–4 minutes per side with Flip Pan closed.

Spread goat cheese on the flatbread and top with Mozzarella cheese.

Take the mushrooms from Flip Pan and place on the flat bread.

Apply nonstick to Flip Pan.

Place flatbread in Flip Pan; close lid.

Cook for 3–4 minutes with Flip Pan closed, or until cheese is melted.

Serve immediately.

Prosciutto Wrapped Shrimp

Servings: 2

INGREDIENTS

16 jumbo shrimp, peeled, butterflied and deveined

16 sage leaves

4 ounces goat cheese, cut into 16 thin slices

8 prosciutto slices, cut in half

¼ cup port wine

nonstick cook spray

DIRECTIONS

Fill each shrimp with 1 sage leaf and 1 slice of goat cheese.

Wrap prosciutto around each shrimp.

Slide a bamboo skewer through 2 shrimp.

Spread port wine on shrimp.

Preheat Flip Pan, top and bottom, on medium heat for 2–3 minutes per side.

Apply nonstick to Flip Pan.

Place skewers in Flip Pan; close lid.

Cook for 5 minutes per side and serve.

Juicy Burgers

INGREDIENTS

1 pound ground chuck
½ teaspoon sea salt
½ teaspoon balsamic vinegar
¼ teaspoon freshly ground pepper
½ teaspoon steak sauce

DIRECTIONS

In a bowl, combine all ingredients except steak sauce; mix well.

Form meat into equal size patties.

Brush patties with steak sauce.

Preheat Flip Pan, top and bottom, on medium heat for 2–3 minutes per side.

Place patties into Flip Pan; close lid.

Cook for 5 minutes per side.

Dress with your favorite toppings and serve.

Sundried Tomato Turkey Breast Burgers

Servings: 4

✻ This recipe works in all of the Flip Pans except for the Jumbo.

INGREDIENTS

½ cup julienned sundried tomatoes in oil, drained with ½ tablespoon oil reserved
2 cloves garlic, minced
1 pound ground turkey breast
6 leaves basil, torn
3 tablespoons Parmesan cheese, grated
1 teaspoon sea salt
½ teaspoon freshly ground pepper

DIRECTIONS

Preheat Flip Pan top and bottom over medium heat for 2–3 minutes per side.

Add ½ tablespoon of reserved tomato oil to the pan. Add the garlic and cook for 2 minutes with lid closed.

Remove the garlic from the Flip Pan and place in a large bowl to cool for 5 minutes.

Leave the remaining oil in the Flip Pan and let pan cool until burgers are made.

Add all the remaining ingredients to the bowl.

Gently mix the ingredients with your hands, and then form 4 equal sized burgers.

Again preheat Flip Pan top and bottom over medium-high heat for 2–3 minutes per side.

Add the burgers and cook for 4–5 minutes over medium-high heat.

Flip and cook 4 minutes longer.

Make sure burgers are cooked through. Everyone's stove can differ slightly.

Serve with mayonnaise on a brioche bun with bib lettuce or spinach, avocado, and roasted red peppers.

Yvonne Ouellette Swenson's
Pearl Couscous with Shrimp & Broccoli

Servings: 6

Seasoning can be adjusted according to taste. We like things with a little kick. The seasonings in this recipe left a little heat in the back of our throats—just enough to savor.

INGREDIENTS

1 pound large shrimp, peeled and deveined
2 tablespoons olive oil
1½ cups pearl couscous
3 cups chicken stock
1 red bell pepper, finely diced
2 large shallots, minced
2 large cloves of garlic, finely diced
4–5 cups small broccoli florets
1 tablespoon dried thyme (crushed)
2 teaspoons freshly ground pepper
2 tablespoons butter
salt to taste
juice from 2 lemons
cilantro

DIRECTIONS

Microwave or steam broccoli until al dente. Set aside.

Preheat FP. Add olive oil and diced pepper. Sauté for 2–3 minutes. Add shallots and garlic. Sauté for 1–2 minutes. Add thyme, pepper, and salt. Stir to combine.

Add chicken stock ~ bring to boil. Add Couscous ~ stir to combine ingredients. Reduce heat to medium, cover and cook approximately 5 minutes.

Remove cover, stir in shrimp and broccoli. Return cover and let simmer until liquid is absorbed, approximately 5–7 minutes. Remove cover, add butter and lemon juice, and stir gently.

Garnish with cilantro.

Round Flip Pan

Grilled Italian Hoagies

Servings: 2

INGREDIENTS

extra-virgin olive oil

2 hoagie rolls, split open

¼ cup spicy pickled peppers, chopped (jalapeno, banana, Greek or cherry peppers)

½ teaspoon green olives, chopped

¼ pound Genoa salami, shaved

¼ pound capicola, shaved

¼ pound ham, shaved

1 whole roasted red pepper, chopped and drained

1 slice provolone cheese

1 slice mozzarella cheese

DIRECTIONS

Spread olive oil on all sides of the hoagie rolls.

Preheat Flip Pan top and bottom over medium heat for 2–3 minutes.

Divide all the ingredients in half and stack on each hoagie roll.

Place hoagie in Flip Pan; close lid.

Cook for 3 minutes on each side and serve.

Grilled Swordfish with Pineapple Salsa

Servings: 2

INGREDIENTS

2 swordfish steaks, 1-inch thick

juice and zest from 2 limes, divided

½ cup bottled teriyaki marinade

nonstick spray

4 pineapple rings, fresh or canned

1 small chili pepper, seeded and membrane removed, finely chopped

2 green onions, finely chopped

1 tablespoon fresh cilantro, finely chopped

nonstick cooking spray

DIRECTIONS

Place swordfish, half of lime juice, and marinade in a one-gallon zipper bag. Let marinate for 30 minutes.

Preheat Flip Pan, top and bottom, on medium heat for 2–3 minutes per side.

Spray top and bottom with nonstick spray.

Place pineapple rings in Flip Pan; close lid.

Cook for 3 minutes per side, remove and cut into small pieces.

In a bowl combine pineapple, remaining lime juice, zest, peppers, onions and cilantro to make a salsa.

Apply additional nonstick to Flip Pan.

Place swordfish filets in Flip Pan; close lid.

Cook for 4 minutes per side.

Rotate steaks a quarter turn to achieve diamond grill marks; grill for an additional 4 minutes per side, or desired doneness.

Top with salsa and serve.

Grilled Vegetable Panini

Servings: 2

INGREDIENTS

1 small sweet onion, thinly sliced

1 small eggplant, sliced into ½-inch rounds

1 zucchini, cut into rounds

½ cup Greek Marinade, page 163

1 small red pepper, quartered

2 ciabatta rolls, sliced lengthwise

¼ cup My Favorite Pesto, page 166

¼ cup Italian cheese blend, shredded

DIRECTIONS

In a bowl combine onion, eggplant, red pepper, zucchini slices in the marinade. Marinate for at least 30 minutes.

Preheat Flip Pan, top and bottom, on medium heat for 2–3 minutes per side.

Place all the vegetables in the Flip Pan—try not to overlap; close lid.

Cook for 5 minutes per side or until tender.

Spread the inside bottom of one roll with pesto and layer with half the grilled vegetables and top with half of the cheese. Cover with other ciabatta half.

Repeat last step with remaining ingredients.

Place sandwiches in Flip Pan; close lid.

Cook for 3 minutes per side or until cheese is melted.

Serve immediately.

Grilled Pear Prosciutto Panini

Servings: 2

INGREDIENTS

1 whole pear, cored and thinly sliced lengthwise
1 teaspoon lemon juice
1 tablespoon honey
nonstick cooking spray
4 slices brioche bread
1 tablespoon unsalted butter, softened
2 ounces Brie, sliced
2 ounces Gorgonzola cheese
2 slices prosciutto

DIRECTIONS

In a bowl, combine pears, lemon juice, and honey. Mix well.

Preheat Flip Pan, top and bottom, on medium heat for 2–3 minutes per side.

Spray top and bottom with nonstick spray.

Place pear slices in Flip Pan; close lid.

Cook 3 minutes per side.

Spread one side of each piece of bread with butter, flip over, then top with pears, Brie, Gorgonzola and prosciutto. Cover with other bread slice, butter-side up.

Repeat with remaining ingredients.

Place sandwiches in Flip Pan; close lid.

Cook for 3 minutes per side and serve.

Grilled Red Potatoes

Servings: 4

INGREDIENTS

3 tablespoons extra-virgin olive oil

10 small red potatoes, sliced ¼-inch thick

1 teaspoon kosher salt

½ teaspoon freshly ground pepper

½ teaspoon rosemary leaves

DIRECTIONS

Preheat Flip Pan, top and bottom, on medium heat for 2–3 minutes per side.

Add the oil to the Flip Pan and let heat for 3 minutes.

Place potato slices in Flip Pan, season with salt, pepper, and rosemary, and mix well.
Close lid.

Cook for 10 minutes per side shaking Flip Pan occasionally.

Grilled Lobster Tails

Servings: 2

INGREDIENTS

2 lobster tails, 6 ounces each
½ tablespoon olive oil
¼ teaspoon sea salt
½ teaspoon seafood seasoning
1 tablespoon butter
1 tablespoon fresh lemon juice
1 tablespoon dry white wine

DIRECTIONS

Using kitchen shears, butterfly the lobster tails straight down the middle of the softer underside of the shell. Cut the meat down the center, without cutting all the way through. Insert a skewer down the lobster tail so the tail stands straight. Brush the tails with olive oil and season with salt and seafood seasoning.

Preheat Flip Pan, top and bottom, on medium heat for 2–3 minutes per side.

Place the lobster meat side down on the grill surface, close lid and let cook for 2–3 minutes.

Add the butter, lemon juice and white wine. Close Flip Pan and cook 4 minutes longer, or until lobster meat is cooked through.

Serve with the butter on the side for dipping.

Eggplant Stacks

Servings: 2

INGREDIENTS

1 cup Parmesan cheese, grated

½ teaspoon Italian seasoning

1 large egg, beaten

1 medium eggplant, sliced into ½-inch rounds

nonstick cooking spray

1 tablespoon olive oil

1 cup baby heirloom tomatoes, halved (or substitute grape tomatoes)

½ teaspoon sea salt

1 ball burrata cheese, sliced

4 basil leaves, chopped

1 tablespoon balsamic reduction

DIRECTIONS

Spread Parmesan cheese and Italian seasoning on a plate.

Pour egg into a bowl

Dip eggplant into egg and roll in Parmesan mixture.

Preheat Flip Pan, top and bottom, on medium heat for 2–3 minutes per side.

Apply nonstick spray to Flip Pan.

Place eggplant slices in Flip Pan; close lid.

Cook for 3 minutes per side.

Remove the eggplant to a platter, add the olive oil to the Flip Pan and heat for 2 minutes.

Add the tomatoes and sea salt. Close lid and cook for 3 minutes, shaking Flip Pan occasionally.

Assemble stacks by alternating eggplant slices and cheese, then a few tomatoes, another eggplant slice then top with more tomatoes, sprinkle with chopped basil and drizzle with balsamic reduction.

Serve immediately.

Monte Cristo Sandwich

Servings: 2

INGREDIENTS

4 slices challah bread, sliced 1-inch thick
½ pound lean ham, shaved
½ pound turkey breast, shaved
2 slices Swiss cheese
2 ounces Brie
2 large eggs, beaten
½ cup heavy cream
nonstick spray

DIRECTIONS

Top one challah slice with half of all the ham, turkey, Swiss cheese and Brie; cover with other challah slice. Repeat with remaining sandwich ingredients.

In a bowl, combine eggs and cream; mix well.

Soak sandwich in egg mixture.

Preheat Flip Pan, top and bottom, on medium heat for 2–3 minutes per side.

Spray Flip Pan with nonstick spray.

Place sandwich in Flip Pan; close and cook for 4 minutes on each side.

Serve immediately.

Filet Mignon with Gorgonzola

Servings: 2

INGREDIENTS

2 tablespoons extra-virgin olive oil

1 garlic clove, minced

1 small shallot, minced

2 filet mignon, 4–5 ounces each

½ teaspoon sea salt

½ teaspoon freshly ground pepper

¼ cup dry red wine

¼ cup beef stock

2 tablespoons Gorgonzola cheese, crumbled

DIRECTIONS

Preheat a Flip Pan on medium heat for 2–3 minutes.

Add the oil and let heat for a minute.

Add garlic and shallots to the Flip Pan and close lid and cook for 2 minutes or until translucent. Do not brown.

Scrape mixture from the pan and set aside.

Rub steaks with sea salt and pepper, add to the Flip Pan. Cook with Flip Pan open for 4 minutes, turn the steaks with tongs and cook with Flip Pan open for another 4 minutes.

Add the shallot mixture, wine and stock to the Flip Pan; close lid and cook for 2 minutes.

Open the Flip Pan and add the gorgonzola to the tops of the steaks, close the pan and cook for 1 minute longer or until the cheese begins to melt.

Grilled Cheese with Bacon and Heirloom Tomatoes

Servings: 1–2

INGREDIENTS

2 thick slices bacon

½ tablespoon mayonnaise

2 slices English muffin bread

1 slice Jarlsburg cheese

1 slice provolone

1 slice ripe heirloom tomato

1 slice cheddar cheese

DIRECTIONS

Preheat Flip Pan top and bottom over medium heat for 2–3 minutes per side.

Place bacon in Flip Pan and lower lid.

Grill for 3–5 minutes or until desired doneness; transfer bacon to paper towels to drain excess fat.

Spread mayonnaise on both sides of each bread slice.

Top 1 bread slice with Jarlsburg and provolone cheeses, bacon, tomato, then cheddar cheese; cover with other bread slice.

Place sandwich in Flip Pan and close the lid.

Grill for 2 minutes on each side, or until cheese is melted and golden brown.

Serve immediately.

Cornbread Stuffed Pork Chops

Servings: 2

INGREDIENTS

½ cup cornbread stuffing, divided
2 pork chops, 1-inch thick, butterflied
½ tablespoon olive oil
½ teaspoon salt
¼ teaspoon freshly ground pepper
¼ teaspoon ground fennel
¼ cup chicken stock

DIRECTIONS

Prepare cornbread stuffing.

Fill each pork chop with stuffing and secure with toothpick.

Rub pork chops with olive oil and season with salt, pepper, and fennel.

Preheat Flip Pan, top and bottom, on medium heat for 2–3 minutes per side.

Place pork chops in Flip Pan; close lid.

Cook for 6 minutes; flip. Then add chicken stock to pan, close and cook for 6 minutes longer.

Crunchy Mahi-Mahi

Servings: 2

INGREDIENTS

2 mahi-mahi filets, 5 ounces each
1 teaspoon mayonnaise
½ cup macadamia nuts
¼ cup panko crumbs
¼ cup coconut, shredded and toasted
2 tablespoons coconut oil

DIRECTIONS

Rub filets with mayonnaise.

In a food processor, combine nuts, panko crumbs, and coconut; process for 30 seconds.

Spread mixture on a plate and press filets into mixture.

Preheat Flip Pan top and bottom over medium heat.

Add the coconut oil and close lid and heat for 3 minutes longer.

Place filets in Flip Pan; close lid. Cook for 3 minutes.

Flip and cook for 3–4 minutes longer.

Daniel Green's Jumbo Party Burger

Servings: 12

If you wish to make the giant roll yourself, use 2 1-pound packages of white bread mix and follow the instructions on the package, then press into Round flip pan and bake in the oven until cooked through, approximately 25 minutes. Brush with egg whites, and sprinkle with sesame seeds if you like.

INGREDIENTS

3 pounds lean ground beef

3 tablespoons ketchup

3 large eggs

3 tablespoons Dijon mustard

1 large red onion, finely chopped

3 cloves garlic, crushed

3 teaspoons salt

3 teaspoons pepper

3 teaspoons onion powder (optional)

3 teaspoons cayenne pepper

3 tablespoons chopped fresh parsley

DIRECTIONS

Mix all the ingredients together with your hands in a bowl.

Line the top and bottom of the round flip pan with plastic wrap.

Place the ground meat mixture into the pan and form to pan.

For best flavor development, wrap the burger in plastic wrap and let rest overnight in refrigerator, or for at least 1 hour.

Preheat Round Flip Pan, top and bottom, over medium heat for 3 minutes per side.

Add the giant burger and cook for 5 minutes per side over medium-high heat.

Drain off any fat.

Serve on a giant bun and layer your choice of cheese, onion, lettuce and even guacamole.

Classic Potato Pancake

Servings: 2

INGREDIENTS

2 large russet potatoes, washed and peeled
2 tablespoons extra-virgin olive oil
nonstick spray
1 teaspoon salt, divided

DIRECTIONS

Shred potatoes with box grater, processor, or spiral vegetable slicer.

Squeeze potatoes with paper towels to remove excess water.

Preheat Round Flip Pan, top and bottom, on medium heat for 2–3 minutes per side.

Pour oil into Flip Pan, let heat for 2 minutes, and spray the lid with nonstick spray.

Add potatoes to pan forming a large pancake, sprinkle with salt.

Close lid and let cook for 3–4 minutes.

Flip, open and add a sprinkle of salt. Close and cook another 4 minutes.

Delicious served topped with Crème fraiche and smoked salmon and capers. Cut like a pizza and serve.

Chipotle Cheeseburgers

Servings: 2

Add some adobo sauce to your mayonnaise or ketchup for this burger . . . caliente!!!

INGREDIENTS

½ pound ground chuck

¼ teaspoon chipotle chili powder

1 tablespoon onion, minced

1 tablespoon canned chipotle in adobo sauce, chopped

¼ teaspoon vinegar

¼ cup Monterey pepper-jack cheese, shredded

2 brioche hamburger buns, toasted

2 lettuce leaves

¼ cup salsa

4 avocados, sliced

DIRECTIONS

In a bowl, combine chuck, chili powder, onion, chilies, vinegar and cheese; mix well.

Form meat into equal sized patties.

Preheat Flip Pan over medium heat 2–3 minutes per side.

Place patties in Flip Pan; close lid.

Cook for 6 minutes per side, or until desired doneness.

Top each bottom bun with lettuce, salsa, and avocado slices.

Serve on prepared buns.

Roast Beef Panini

Servings: 2

INGREDIENTS

1 tablespoon unsalted butter

1 large shallot, thinly sliced

pinch of fresh thyme

pinch of salt

pinch of freshly ground pepper

1 teaspoon horseradish sauce

1 small baguette, sliced lengthwise

½ pound medium-rare roast beef, thinly sliced

¼ cup Gorgonzola cheese, crumbled

DIRECTIONS

Preheat Flip Pan top and bottom over medium heat for 2–3 minutes per side.

Add butter to the flat side of Flip Pan and let melt.

Add shallot, thyme, salt and pepper to pan; sauté until golden brown.

Spread horseradish on bottom baguette half.

Top baguette with roast beef, shallot mixture and cheese, place baguette back in Flip Pan, grill side down; close lid and cook 4 minutes each side, or until cheese is melted and bread is toasted.

Chicken Parmesan

Servings: 2

INGREDIENTS

nonstick cooking spray

1 large egg, beaten

½ cup Parmesan cheese, shredded

2 boneless, skinless chicken breasts

½ teaspoon Italian seasoning

2 slices fresh mozzarella cheese

2 cups Marinara Sauce, page 166

DIRECTIONS

Preheat Flip Pan, top and bottom, on medium heat for 2–3 minutes per side.

Spray top and bottom with nonstick spray.

Pour egg into a bowl.

Spread Parmesan cheese on a plate.

Dip chicken into egg and roll in Parmesan cheese until coated.

Sprinkle Italian seasoning over chicken.

Place chicken breasts in Flip Pan; close lid.

Cook 5 minutes per side, or until cooked through; remove.

Top each chicken breast with 1 slice mozzarella cheese.

Pour the Marinara Sauce into the Flip Pan and close lid heat for 3 minutes.

Place chicken breasts in Flip Pan; close lid.

Cook an additional 2 minutes.

Chicken with Mango Salsa

Servings: 2

INGREDIENTS

4 boneless, skinless chicken thighs
1 cup jerk marinade
1 teaspoon Jerk Rub, page 165
nonstick cooking spray
1 cup Mango Salsa, page 164

DIRECTIONS

Place chicken and marinade into a one-gallon zipper bag; let marinate for 1 hour.

Season chicken with Jerk Rub.

Preheat Flip Pan, top and bottom, on medium heat for 2–3 minutes per side.

Apply nonstick spray to Flip Pan.

Place chicken in Flip Pan; close lid.

Cook for 8–10 minutes per side or until chicken is cooked through.

Top chicken with Mango Salsa and serve.

Fantastic served with black beans and rice.

Buttermilk Pancakes

Servings: 2

This is fun as one great big pancake!

INGREDIENTS

½ cup all-purpose flour
2 teaspoons sugar
½ teaspoon baking powder
pinch of baking soda
pinch of salt
1 egg, beaten
1 teaspoon vanilla extract
½ cup buttermilk or yogurt
1 tablespoon butter, at room temperature
nonstick spray

DIRECTIONS

Preheat Flip Pan, top and bottom, on medium heat for 2–3 minutes per side.

In a large bowl, combine flour, sugar, baking powder, baking soda, and salt; mix well and form a well in the center of the bowl.

In a separate bowl, combine egg, vanilla, buttermilk, and butter.

Gently pour the liquid into the flour mixture; stir to incorporate, do not overmix.

Spray Flip Pan top and bottom with nonstick spray.

Ladle pancake batter onto griddle side of Flip Pan and spread to desired thickness; close lid.

Cook for 2–3 minutes, flip and cook for 2 minutes longer or until cooked through.

Serve hot with butter and maple syrup.

Cannoli Panini

Servings: 2

INGREDIENTS

½ cup whole milk ricotta cheese

2 tablespoons powdered sugar

1 teaspoon almond extract

½ cup whipped cream (store bought or homemade)

2 teaspoons butter, softened

4 slices pound cake, cut ½-inch thick

2 tablespoons mini chocolate morsels, divided

powdered sugar, for dusting.

DIRECTIONS

In a food processor, combine cheese, sugar, and extract; process until smooth.

Fold in the whipped cream.

Preheat Flip Pan, top and bottom, on medium heat for 2–3 minutes per side.

Spread butter on 1 side of each pound cake slice and place them butter-side down on a cutting board.

Top 2 cake slices with cheese mixture and morsels; cover with other cake slices, butter side up.

Place cannoli in Flip Pan; close lid.

Cook for 2 minutes per side.

Dust cannoli with remaining powdered sugar and serve.

Black Forest Chocolate Crepes

Servings: 2

INGREDIENTS

2 large eggs
½ cup water
½ cup heavy cream
½ cup all-purpose flour
1 tablespoon cocoa powder
3 tablespoons sugar
pinch salt
2 tablespoons unsalted butter, room temperature
butter-flavored nonstick spray
cherry pie filling
chocolate fudge sauce
whipped cream

DIRECTIONS

Preheat Flip Pan, top and bottom, on medium heat for 2–3 minutes per side.

In a food processor, combine eggs, water, cream, flour, cocoa, sugar, salt and butter; process for 10 seconds or until smooth.

Apply nonstick spray to Flip Pan top and bottom.

Ladle 3 tablespoons of batter into griddle side; spread batter with the back of the ladle to form 5-inch circles. Close lid.

Cook for 2 minutes per side.

Top crepe with 1 tablespoon of cherry pie filling and fold it into a triangle; drizzle with fudge sauce and top with whipped cream.

Repeat steps with remaining ingredients and serve.

Blueberry French Toast

Servings: 2

INGREDIENTS

3 large eggs, beaten
½ cup milk
1 teaspoon sugar
1 teaspoon vanilla
pinch of salt
4 slices challah bread, cut 1½-inches thick
butter-flavored nonstick spray
1–2 cups blueberry topping

DIRECTIONS

Preheat Flip Pan, top and bottom, on medium heat for 2–3 minutes per side.

In a bowl, combine eggs, milk, sugar, vanilla, and salt; mix well.

Place bread slices in bowl, let soak for 1 minute.

Apply nonstick spray to Flip Pan.

Place French toast in Flip Pan; close lid.

Cook 4 minutes on one side, 2 minutes on the other.

Serve with blueberry topping.

BBQ Chicken Quesadillas

Servings: 2

INGREDIENTS

1 teaspoon extra-virgin olive oil

2 boneless, skinless chicken breasts, 4 ounces each

2 tablespoons Barbecue Rub, page 165

1 small onion, sliced

2 tablespoons canned diced green chilies

½ cup Barbecue Sauce, page 165

1 tablespoon mayonnaise

4 flour tortillas, 6 inches in diameter

½ cup Mexican cheese blend, shredded

DIRECTIONS

Preheat Flip Pan top and bottom over medium heat for 2–3 minutes.

Rub oil on chicken and season with Barbecue Rub.

Place chicken in Flip Pan; close lid.

Cook for 4 minutes then flip. Open Flip Pan and add in the onions and green chilies. Close lid and cook 4 minutes longer.

Remove chicken and vegetables to platter, while keeping Flip Pan warm.

Cut chicken into cubes and toss with vegetables and the Barbecue Sauce.

Spread mayonnaise on 1 side of each tortilla and place them mayonnaise-side down on a cutting board.

Divide chicken mixture and cheese between 2 tortillas; cover with remaining tortillas, mayonnaise-side up.

Place quesadillas in Flip Pan; close lid.

Cook for 3 minutes per side, cut into fourths and serve.

Josephine Cook's Homemade Manicotti

Servings: 3

INGREDIENTS

1 pound ricotta cheese

¼ cup Parmesan cheese (plus more for garnishing)

3 tablespoons fresh parsley, chopped

2 eggs

salt and pepper, to taste

1 cup flour

1 cup water

4 cups Marinara Sauce, page 166, or bottled Pasta sauce

oil for making the manicotti shell

DIRECTIONS

Preheat oven to 350 degrees.

In a bowl add ricotta cheese, parmesan cheese, parsley, 1 egg and season with salt and pepper, and mix it. Set aside.

In a mixing bowl, add flour, water, 1 egg, pinch of salt and some pepper. With a hand beater, mix until smooth. This is the mainicotti batter.

Take the Round Flip Pan apart. With some oil on a paper towel, wipe the inside of the pan and heat on the stove, medium heat, until hot.

Take one scoop of a medium-sized ladle of the shell batter and pour it into the hot pan. Rotate the pan, so the batter spreads out to make a thin shell.

When it starts to curl around the sides, flip the shell with a fork, cook for a few seconds longer—just to dry the top side of the shell. Remove and place on a parchment-lined platter to cool.

Continue this process until all the batter is used. Makes 6 medium-large shells. You can make them any size you like.

In the center of each shell, add a heaping spoonful of the ricotta mixture and roll the shell around it.

In the grill side of the round Flip Pan, add some pasta sauce and spread evenly in the pan.

Add the filled manicotti.

Top with more pasta sauce and parmesan cheese.

Place the glass lid on the pan and place in the oven. Bake 350 degrees for 30 minutes. The sauce will begin to bubble. Remove the lid, and bake for 10 minutes. (Use a pot holder, the handle and lid are hot.)

Let sit for a few minutes to settle and serve with more Parmesan cheese and pasta sauce.

Baby Back Ribs

Servings: 2

INGREDIENTS

½ slab baby back ribs
½ tablespoon extra-virgin olive oil
1 tablespoon Barbecue Rub, page 165
nonstick cooking spray
¼ cup chicken stock

DIRECTIONS

Preheat Flip Pan, top and bottom, on medium heat for 2–3 minutes per side.

Rub ribs with oil and Barbecue Rub.

Apply nonstick spray to Flip Pan.

Place ribs in Flip Pan, meat side down; close lid.

Cook for 10 minutes. Flip and add the chicken stock, close and cook over medium for 15 minutes longer.

Bacon Wrapped Shrimp

Servings: 2

INGREDIENTS

16 jumbo shrimp, butterflied
½ cup Italian dressing
16 chunks Monterey jack cheese
1 serrano pepper, thinly sliced
cilantro leaves
16 bacon strips, cooked
Barbecue Sauce, page 165

DIRECTIONS

Place shrimp and dressing into a one-gallon zipper bag and let marinate for 30 minutes.

Place shrimp, seam-side down, on a cutting board.

Stuff 1 shrimp with a piece of cheese and pepper and a couple cilantro leaves; close shrimp, wrap it with a piece of bacon and secure with a toothpick.

Repeat with remaining shrimp.

Preheat Flip Pan top and bottom over medium heat for 2 minutes per side.

Place shrimp in Flip Pan; close lid.

Cook for 4 minutes, flip and cook for 3 minutes longer.

Serve with Barbecue Sauce for dipping.

Baby Artichokes

Servings: 2

INGREDIENTS

8 baby artichokes, halved lengthwise
1 cup Greek Marinade, page 163
2 tablespoons mayonnaise
¼ cup dry white wine

DIRECTIONS

In a bowl, combine artichokes and marinade; let marinate for 1 hour.

Preheat Flip Pan, top and bottom, on medium heat for 2–3 minutes per side.

Rub mayonnaise on the flat side of each artichoke.

Place artichokes in Flip Pan; close lid.

Cook for 3 minutes, flip, then add wine and cook 5 minutes longer.

Delicious hot or cold.

Asparagus and Brie Panini

Servings: 1–2

INGREDIENTS

4 medium asparagus spears, washed and trimmed
½ teaspoon lemon juice
pinch of salt
½ teaspoon My Favorite Pesto, page 166
1 small French baguette, sliced lengthwise
4 slices prosciutto
2 ounces Brie, sliced into ¼-inch slices
nonstick cook spray

DIRECTIONS

Preheat Flip Pan, top and bottom, on medium heat for 2–3 minutes per side.

In a bowl, combine asparagus, lemon juice and salt; toss well.

Place asparagus into Flip Pan; close lid.

Cook for 3 minutes per side.

Transfer asparagus to a platter, cut into 2-inch pieces.

Spread pesto onto bottom baguette half; top with prosciutto, asparagus, and Brie and cover with other baguette half.

Apply nonstick spray to Flip Pan.

Place sandwich in Flip Pan; close lid.

Cook for 3 minutes per side and serve.

Apple Pie French Toast

Servings: 2

INGREDIENTS

2 large eggs, beaten
½ cup half and half
4 slices cinnamon bread
½ cup apple filling
2 tablespoons honey nut cream cheese, softened
½ teaspoon cinnamon
nonstick cooking spray

DIRECTIONS

Preheat Flip Pan, top and bottom, on medium heat for 2–3 minutes per side.

In a bowl, whisk together the eggs and half and half.

Add bread slices to the bowl and let soak.

Top 1 bread slice with ¼ cup apple pie filling and 1 tablespoon cream cheese.

Top with cinnamon and cover with other bread slice.

Repeat steps with remaining ingredients.

Apply nonstick to Flip Pan top and bottom.

Place French toast in Flip Pan; close lid.

Cook for 2–3 minutes on each side and serve.

Zucchini Pancake

Servings: 2

INGREDIENTS

4 large eggs
½ teaspoon sea salt
¼ teaspoon fresh ground pepper
2 green onions, chopped fine
½ cup shredded zucchini, drained
1 tablespoon Parmesan cheese, grated
nonstick spray
8 grape tomatoes, quartered
6 basil leaves torn

DIRECTIONS

Preheat the Round Flip Pan top and bottom over medium heat for 2–3 minutes per side.

In a large bowl beat the eggs, then add in all the remaining ingredients except the tomatoes and basil. Mix well.

Spray the Round Flip Pan top and bottom with nonstick spray, then add the batter to the pan and close.

Cook for 3 minutes over medium high. Then flip the Flip Pan and cook for 4 minutes longer.

Open and ensure the pancake is cooked through.

Remove the top of the round Flip Pan and invert zucchini pancake onto a platter.

Top with diced tomatoes and basil and serve at once.

Josephine Cook's Zucchini Sticks

Servings: 4

INGREDIENTS

1 tablespoon extra-virgin olive oil

2 large zucchini or yellow squash

¼ cup Panko crumbs or bread crumbs

¼ cup grated Romano cheese or parmesan cheese

¼ teaspoon each salt, pepper, garlic powder; or use
what you like—onion powder, Mrs. Dash seasonings,
or even some cayenne pepper for a kick

non-stick cooking spray

DIRECTIONS

Cut the zucchini in half lengthwise, and then into ¼-inch sticks.

In a bowl add the oil, and then the zucchini. Mix to coat on both sides.

In another bowl, mix the Panko or breadcrumbs, Romano cheese and the seasonings of your choice.

Open the Flip Pan, spritz with olive oil or spray

Shut the lid and preheat for 4 minutes on each side on medium low heat.

Dip the zucchini into the Panko mixture, coating both sides and place in the Flip Pan. I did not use the grill side. Really does not matter.

Close the lid and cook for 8 minutes.

Open the lid and turn them by hand. If you flip, they will all slide together—yes, I tried.

Close the lid and cook 3 more minutes. They are crisp tender. Cook longer if you like them softer.

Mediterranean Chicken Panini

Servings: 2

INGREDIENTS

¾ cup Greek Marinade, page 163

2 medium boneless, skinless chicken breasts, trimmed of fat

1 loaf Italian bread, sliced lengthwise

¼ cup sun-dried tomato pesto

4 artichoke hearts, thinly sliced

2 ounces garlic herb cheese spread

½ cup arugula

DIRECTIONS

In a bowl, combine marinade and chicken; let marinate in the refrigerator for 1 hour.

Preheat Flip Pan top and bottom over medium heat for 2–3 minutes per side.

Place marinated chicken in Flip Pan; close lid.

Cook for 7 minutes per side.

Transfer chicken to cutting board and slice diagonally into strips.

Spread the inside of the loaf with pesto.

Top bottom half of loaf with chicken, artichoke hearts, and cheese; cover with other half of bread.

Place sandwich in Flip Pan; close lid.

Cook for 4 minutes on each side.

Add arugula to sandwich and serve.

Laurie Bain's Snapper Vera Cruz

Servings: 2

INGREDIENTS

2 tablespoons extra-virgin olive oil

2 snapper filets, 4 ounces each

1 teaspoon sea salt, divided

½ teaspoon fresh ground pepper

1 medium onion, sliced thin

1 green bell pepper, julienned

2 cloves garlic, minced

1 14.5-ounce can diced tomatoes

1 tablespoon fresh lime juice

2 tablespoons fresh cilantro, chopped

1 teaspoon green olives, chopped

2 green onions, chopped

DIRECTIONS

Preheat Flip Pan, top and bottom, on medium heat for 2–3 minutes per side.

Add the olive oil and heat for 2 minutes.

Season snapper with half the salt and all of the pepper.

Add the snapper to the Flip Pan, close the lid, and cook for 3 minutes.

Flip and cook for 3 minutes longer. Remove the fish from the pan to a platter and reserve.

Add the onion and pepper to the Flip Pan, close and cook for 3 minutes.

Add the garlic, close and cook for 2 minutes more.

Stir in the tomatoes and the rest of the salt. Close Flip Pan and cook 3 minutes longer.

Stir in the lime juice, cilantro and olives, top with the snapper and close the Flip Pan and cook for 3 minutes longer.

Garnish with green onions and serve.

Jumbo Flip Pan

Georgina Budney's Sticky Chicken Wings

Servings: 4

INGREDIENTS

3 boneless, skinless chicken breasts

½ cup all-purpose flour

1 cup panko

2 eggs

2 tablespoons water

1½ cups brown sugar

2 tablespoons canola oil

1 tablespoon water

⅓ cup hot sauce

½ teaspoon garlic powder

DIRECTIONS

Slice breasts into strips.

In a bowl or bag, add chicken to flour and coat.

Place panko crumbs in a bowl. In another bowl whisk eggs and water.

Dip chicken in egg then panko.

Heat large Flip Pan on stove on medium heat. Put canola oil in pan.

Heat Flip Pan with oil for additional 3 minutes over medium heat. When heated, place strips in pan.

Close Flip Pan and cook for two minutes.

Turn the chicken pieces, then close lid and cook for 2 minutes longer.

When lightly browned on each side, shut heat off. Remove chicken to a paper towel to drain.

In the small Flip Pan or a sauce pan, preheat over medium.

Add the brown sugar, hot sauce, and garlic powder in pan and stir. When it starts to boil, add water and stir. Remove from the heat.

Dredge chicken in sauce. Put back in pan.

Garnish with chopped green onions and serve with ranch dressing.

Jackie Austin's Gluten-Free Chicken Piccata

Servings: 4

This dish goes well with cooked quinoa or angel hair rice pasta, along with asparagus, artichokes, or broccoli. It also can be served with spiralized, cooked zucchini.

INGREDIENTS

4 boneless, skinless chicken breasts (approximately 1 ¼ pounds)

¼ cup quinoa flour

½ teaspoon salt, or to taste

¼ teaspoon black pepper, or to taste

1½ tablespoons coconut oil (or other cooking oil of choice)

3 tablespoons lemon juice (juice of one large or 2 small lemons)

1 cup chicken stock, reduced sodium

½ cup white wine

3 tablespoons arrowroot plus 3 tablespoons cool water, mixed

3 tablespoons capers, to taste

salt and pepper to season sauce, to taste

1 tablespoon butter

½ teaspoon flat-leaf parsley, finely chopped, for garnish

Place each chicken breast between two pieces of waxed paper or parchment, and gently pound with a kitchen mallet to a thickness of ¼ inch. Or use thin-sliced, boneless, skinless chicken breasts.

Mix quinoa flour, salt and pepper. Spread on a plate, then dredge breasts in the quinoa mixture.

Heat coconut oil in grill side of Flip Pan over medium high heat, then add the dredged chicken and sauté for approximately 3 minutes on each side until golden brown and no longer pink inside.

Place cooked chicken in covered dish while preparing piccata sauce.

Without cleaning the Flip Pan, add white wine, lemon juice and chicken stock over medium heat, stirring to loosen the brown bits from the bottom of the pan.

Make a slurry by mixing the arrowroot and water, and add to the pan, while continually stirring.

Add capers and continue stirring for approximately 1 minute, then close the lid, cooking over medium heat 5 minutes until sauce thickens a little more.

Add salt and pepper to the sauce, a little at a time, until desired seasoning is reached.

Add the chicken back to the Flip Pan and cook 3–4 minutes to completely reheat and allow sauce to thicken a little more.

Remove the chicken to serving platter.

Add butter to the remaining sauce in the pan and mix thoroughly. Pour sauce over the chicken.

Garnish with chopped parsley.

Dark Chocolate Marshmallow Nut Fudge

Yield: Makes 1 ¾ pounds

INGREDIENTS

3 cups sugar

¾ cup dark cocoa powder

⅛ teaspoon sea salt

1½ cups milk

¼ cup unsalted butter

1 teaspoon vanilla extract

1 cup marshmallow cream

1 cup walnuts

DIRECTIONS

Line a square baking dish with parchment paper.

Mix sugar and cocoa and salt in the jumbo Flip Pan base, stir in the milk.

Cook mixture over medium heat stirring constantly, until mixture comes to a full boil.

Do not stir after this point. Add candy thermometer and cook mixture until it reads 234 degrees.

Remove the Flip Pan from the hot burner; add in the vanilla and butter and marshmallow cream. Do not stir.

When the candy thermometer reads 110 degrees, beat with a wooden spoon until fudge starts to thicken. About 7 minutes.

Stir in the nuts, quickly spread into prepared pan, and cool completely.

Cut into desired squares and store in an airtight container.

Michael Caldwell Charlotte's Pork Goulash with Sauerkraut

Servings: 4

INGREDIENTS

1½ lbs. boneless pork chops, ½-inch thick,
    cut into cubes and seasoned with salt and pepper

1 medium onion, sliced thin

1 32-ounce jar of sauerkraut, drained

1½ cups sour cream

1 teaspoon salt

¼ teaspoon pepper

¼ teaspoon paprika

3 tablespoons vegetable oil

DIRECTIONS

Preheat Jumbo Flip Pan over medium heat.

Add oil.

Add pork and brown on both sides, lid open.

Reduce heat to medium low.

Add onions.

Add salt, pepper and paprika and stir.

Close lid and cook for 15 minutes, cooking pork and softening onions.

Open lid, stir, add sauerkraut and stir to incorporate it all together.

Close lid and cook for another 15 minutes for flavors to blend.

Open lid, add sour cream and stir through.

Serve immediately over noodles or rice.

Pamela D. Jones Lawson's Favorite Tomato Pudding

Servings: 6

Good served with roast or chicken.

INGREDIENTS

½ cup butter

2 28-ounce cans petite diced tomatoes

5 slices bread, cubed and toasted

2 tablespoons sugar

½ teaspoon allspice

¼ teaspoon salt

¼ teaspoon pepper

DIRECTIONS

Preheat Jumbo Flip Pan over medium heat for 2 minutes.

Add the butter and allow to melt.

Add the remaining ingredients except the bread; close Flip Pan and cook for 20 minutes.

Add toasted bread, cover and simmer covered 10 minutes longer.

Mary Osborne Hamilton's Chicken Veggie Kebabs

Servings: 2

INGREDIENTS

2 boneless, skinless chicken breasts, cut into diced pieces

1 green pepper, cut into 1-inch chunks

1 yellow pepper, cut into 1-inch chunks

1 red pepper, cut into 1-inch chunks

1 orange pepper, cut into 1-inch chunks

1 medium onion, cut into 1-inch chunks

1 8-ounce can pineapple chunks, drained

4 cherry tomatoes

1 bottle teriyaki or Hawaiian marinade

1 teaspoon canola oil

bottle of teriyaki glaze

DIRECTIONS

Assemble chicken pieces, diced peppers, onion, tomatoes; evenly thread onto six skewers.

Place skewers in a rectangle baking dish and cover with marinade. Cover and refrigerate overnight.

Preheat Jumbo Flip Pan lid over medium heat for a couple of minutes.

Add the oil to the lid and spread around and allow to heat for 2 minutes.

Brush the skewers with the glaze, then place in the pan.

Cook kebabs 20 minutes, 10 minutes on each side, on medium heat.

Serve with Rice Pilaf and green salad.

Poached Peaches with Raspberries

Servings: 4

INGREDIENTS

2 cups water

1½ cups sugar

¾ cup Pinot Grigio white wine

¼ teaspoon sea salt

1 cinnamon stick

1 lemon, juice and zest

4 ripe peaches, halved and pitted

1 cup raspberries

DIRECTIONS

Place all the ingredients except the peaches and raspberries in the Flip Pan.

Bring the liquid to a boil over medium high heat.

Carefully place peach halves, skin side up in the Flip Pan.

Close Flip Pan and cook for 8 minutes.

When cooking time is through, remove Flip Pan from stove, add the raspberries without stirring and let cool for 30 minutes.

Strain the peaches through a fine sieve reserving the liquid and slipping off the peaches' skins.

Chill peaches and reserved liquid for at least 2 hours.

Delicious in a bowl on their own with some of the poaching liquid, or serve over ice cream.

Tricia Reynolds Seasoned Chicken Livers

Servings: 2

Serve with ketchup, mayonnaise, or Miracle Whip, if desired.

INGREDIENTS

1-pound container chicken liver

2 cups all-purpose flour

2 tablespoons weber beer can chicken seasonings
   (or 2 tablespoons favorite seasoning for chicken)

2–4 tablespoons canola oil

salt, optional

DIRECTIONS

Trim fat, if any, from chicken livers. Clean livers by rinsing then under cool running water, and drain in a colander.

Using a one-gallon zipper bag, add flour and chicken seasoning, mixing ingredients thoroughly.

One by one, place chicken livers in bag with flour and seasoning. Seal bag shut, leaving some air in the bag.

Flip bag over and over, making sure to coat all livers well.

Add desired amount of canola oil to Flip Pan.

Place Flip Pan on stove top, and heat oil over a medium heat.

When oil is hot, (about 4 minutes) place chicken livers, one at a time, in pan.

Close lid, and cook on medium heat about 3 minutes on each side, until desired doneness.

Serve immediately, as an appetizer or main course meal.

Bucatini Puttanesca

This is such a fabulous pasta on its own. But if you want to add shrimp or mussels, 8 minutes into the cooking process, stir in 1 pound of shrimp or mussels.

INGREDIENTS

4 cups chicken stock
2 cloves of garlic, sliced
1 tablespoon olive oil
½ cup black olives, pitted and thinly sliced
½ cup green olives, pitted and thinly sliced
3 tablespoons capers
1 pound bucatini, pasta
½ teaspoon dried, oregano
1 14.5 ounce can fire roasted petite diced, tomato
1 pint grape, tomato, halved
1 sprig basil
½ teaspoon red pepper, flakes
freshly grated Parmesan cheese

DIRECTIONS

Place the Flip Pan on the Induction burner, add the chicken stock, garlic and olives.

Secure the lid, press power and set on high, set the timer for 8 minutes.

When timer goes off add the remaining ingredients except the parmesan cheese.

Secure the lid and set induction burner to high, set timer for 10 minutes.

At least 1 time during the cooking process open the flip pan and using tongs stir the ingredients to keep pasta from clumping.

Braised Lamb Shanks

Servings: 4

INGREDIENTS

2 tablespoons extra-virgin olive oil

4 (1 pound each) lamb shanks

½ teaspoon salt

½ teaspoon freshly ground pepper

½ cup dry red wine

½ cup chicken stock

2 tablespoons tomato paste

½ cup carrot, diced

1 shallot, minced

3 garlic cloves, minced

½ teaspoon cumin

½ teaspoon coriander

½ teaspoon pumpkin pie spice

1 can (16.5 ounces) petite diced tomato

2 tablespoons fresh cilantro, chopped

DIRECTIONS

Preheat Jumbo Flip Pan over medium heat for several minutes.

Season the lamb shanks with salt and pepper.

Add the oil to the Flip Pan and heat for 2 minutes

Add the lamb shanks. Sear each lamb shank on all sides until browned.

Drain the fat from the pan.

Add remaining ingredients, except cilantro, to the Flip Pan; stir scraping up the browned bits.

Secure Flip Pan lid. Lower heat to medium.

Set a timer for 65 minutes.

When cooking time is complete, top with cilantro, and serve.

Braciole

Servings: 2

INGREDIENTS

1 pound top sirloin, sliced very thin

½ cup unsalted butter, melted

1½ cups Parmesan cheese, grated

1½ soft bread crumbs

1 teaspoon sea salt

½ teaspoon freshly ground pepper

1 tablespoon fresh parsley, chopped

½ teaspoon garlic salt

½ cup raisins

2 tablespoons olive oil

tooth picks

½ cup dry, red wine

1 cup beef stock

1 sprig thyme

3 cups pasta sauce

DIRECTIONS

Lay steak slices on a cutting board.

In a bowl combine butter, cheese, breadcrumbs, salt, pepper, parsley, garlic salt and raisins; mix well.

Place 2 tablespoon raisin mixture on the bottom corner of each steak slice; rollup and secure with a tooth pick.

Preheat Flip Pan over medium heat for 2 minutes, add oil and cook for 1 minute longer.

Add meat rolls to Flip Pan and brown on all sides about 4 minutes.

Add the wine stock and thyme to the Flip Pan, secure the lid and set timer for 30 minutes.

When cooking is complete, remove thyme, add pasta sauce and let sauce heat through.

Serve immediately.

Butternut Squash Soup

Servings: 4

INGREDIENTS

1 large butternut squash, peeled and cut into 1-inch pieces

1 tablespoon extra-virgin olive oil

1 medium onion, diced

2 stalks celery, sliced

1 teaspoon freshly grated ginger

4 cups chicken stock

1 cup apple cider

2 medium apples, peeled and seeded

2 teaspoons curry powder

1 teaspoon sea salt

DIRECTIONS

Preheat the Flip Pan over medium heat for 2 minutes.

Add the oil and heat 1 minute longer.

Add the squash chunks and onions and cook for 3 minutes.

Add in the celery and ginger and cook a couple minutes longer.

Place the remaining ingredients in the Flip Pan and secure the lid.

Set timer for 20 minutes.

When cooking is complete, puree the soup in a blender and serve.

Buttery Corn on the Cob

Servings: 4

INGREDIENTS

8 ears of corn, husked

½ cup water

1 teaspoon salt

½ teaspoon sugar

3 tablespoons butter

2 tablespoons flat leaf parsley, chopped.

DIRECTIONS

Add all the ingredients to the Flip Pan, secure the lid.

Over medium high heat, bring liquid to a boil, about 4 minutes.

Set timer for 6 minutes.

When cooking is complete, stir and serve.

Burgundy Beef

Servings: 6

INGREDIENTS

2 tablespoons olive oil

1 teaspoon sea salt

½ teaspoon freshly ground pepper

1 chuck steak (2 pounds) cut into ½-inch pieces

8 ounces baby Portobello mushrooms, sliced

1 cup beef stock

1 cup pearl onion

4 garlic cloves

3 sprigs fresh thyme

½ cup burgundy wine

¼ cup crushed tomato

2 carrots, peeled and sliced into 2-inch pieces

DIRECTIONS

Place Flip Pan on stove and preheat over medium heat for 2 minutes. Add the oil and heat oil for 2 minutes.

Season steak pieces with salt and pepper.

Place the steak pieces into the Flip Pan with lid off; sear for 2 minutes on each side or until browned. Approximately 8 minutes.

Add the remaining ingredients to the Flip Pan scraping up the browned bits off the bottom of the pan and stirring.

Secure the lid, and set a timer for 60 minutes.

When cooking is complete, discard the thyme and serve immediately.

Caramel Flan

Servings: 4

INGREDIENTS

4 custard cups (5oz)
½ cup sugar
1 tablespoon water
1 cup sweetened condensed milk
1 ¼ cups evaporated milk
3 large eggs yolks
1 teaspoon vanilla

DIRECTIONS

Place the sugar and water in the lid of jumbo Flip Pan over med heat. Cook until sugar turns to caramel. About 3 minutes. Watch constantly so it does not burn.

Pour caramel into the custard cups.

In a mixing bowl, whisk together the milks, yolks, and vanilla.

Divide the mixture between the cups.

Place the rack in the jumbo Flip Pan, and fill Flip Pan with 1 quart of water.

Bring the water to a boil over medium high heat.

Cover each flan with a square of aluminum foil.

Once water comes to a boil, place flans on rack and secure Flip Pan lid.

Set timer for 15 minutes.

Chicken Soup

Servings: 6

INGREDIENTS

4 skinless (but bone in) chicken breasts
6 cups chicken stock
1 teaspoon sea salt
1 teaspoon turmeric powder
1 teaspoon black pepper
1 sprig fresh thyme
1 leek, halved (white part only)
2 garlic cloves
2 celery stalks, cut into 2-inch pieces
2 wholes carrots, peeled and cut into 2-inch pieces
½ cup dry egg noodles
1 tablespoon flat leaf parsley, chopped

DIRECTIONS

Place the chicken, stock, salt, turmeric, pepper, thyme, leeks and garlic into the Flip Pan; secure lid.

Set a timer for 45 minutes.

Remove the chicken, take the meat off the bones, cut up the chicken into 1-inch pieces and add back to the Flip Pan.

Add the celery, carrots, and parsley to the Flip Pan; secure lid.

Set a timer for 10 minutes.

When cooking is complete, stir in egg noodles and cook until tender, about 5 minutes.

Creamy Cheesecakes

Servings: 6

INGREDIENTS

6 4-ounce ramekins or springforms

1½ cups crushed graham crackers

1 tablespoon sugar

½ cup melted butter

2 8-ounce packages cream cheese

1 cup sour cream

1 cup of sugar

2 tablespoons of flour

3 large eggs

1 teaspoon vanilla

1 teaspoon grated lemon peel

1 quart water

DIRECTIONS

Preheat oven to 350 degrees.

Spray the ramekins with nonstick spray.

Combine the graham cracker crumbs with sugar and butter and press into the base of each ramekin. Place in the center rack in the oven and bake for 5 minutes.

Using a food processor or mixer, cream the cream cheese, sour cream, and sugar until very smooth. Add the flour, eggs, vanilla, and lemon peel.

Place the rack in the Flip Pan and add water; bring water to a boil.

Remove the ramekins from the oven and pour in the cheesecake batter.

Wrap each ramekin or springform with aluminum foil.

Place the ramekins on the rack in the Flip Pan. Secure the lid.

Set a timer for 20 minutes.

When cooking time is complete, remove these cheesecakes and refrigerate all of them for at least 1 hour before serving.

BBQ Pulled Pork

Servings: 6

INGREDIENTS

4 pounds boneless pork butt roast
1 teaspoon kosher salt
½ teaspoon freshly ground black pepper
1 cup chicken stock
2 teaspoons soy sauce
2 cups apple cider
1 bottle (16 ounces) barbecue sauce
1 tablespoon cider vinegar
sandwich rolls

DIRECTIONS

Preheat Jumbo Flip Pan over medium high heat.

Season the butt roast with the salt, pepper, and paprika.

Sear the pork roast on all sides.

Add the chicken stock, soy sauce and cider to the Flip Pan.

Secure the Flip Pan lid and cook for 1 hour over medium heat.

Remove the pork from the Flip Pan and cut into 2-inch chunks.

Place the chunks back in the Flip Pan with the barbecue sauce and vinegar.

Secure Flip Pan lid and cook for an additional 30 minutes.

When cooking is complete, serve on sandwich rolls with coleslaw.

Italian Pot Roast

Servings: 4

INGREDIENTS

2 tablespoons extra-virgin olive oil

1 (3–4 pounds) chuck roast

1 teaspoon salt

½ teaspoon freshly ground pepper

¼ cup dry, red wine

1 cup beef stock

1 cup tomato juice

1 medium onion, sliced

3 garlic cloves, sliced

1 bell pepper, diced

1 teaspoon garlic powder

1 teaspoon Italian herb seasoning

½ cup giardiniera spicy pickled vegetable

1 bay leaf

1 bottle (28 ounces) favorite pasta sauce

favorite pasta, cooked

DIRECTIONS

Preheat the Flip Pan over medium heat for 2 minutes. Add the oil and heat 1 minute longer.

Season the chuck roast with salt and pepper.

Add the chuck roast to the Flip Pan and sear for 3 minutes on each side.

Add the wine, tomato juice, and stock to the Flip Pan and scrape up the browned bits off the bottom of the pan.

Add the onions, garlic, bell pepper, garlic powder, Italian seasoning and bay leaf to the Flip Pan; secure lid.

Bring Flip Pan to a boil, about 10 minutes. Lower heat to medium and set a timer for 90 minutes.

When cooking is complete, remove the bay leaf and place the roast on a platter.

With lid open, reduce the cooking liquid by half, about 5 or 6 minutes, then add the pasta sauce and stir.

Pour sauce over roast and serve with favorite pasta or on a hoagie roll with provolone cheese.

Lentil Turkey Sausage Soup

Servings: 4

INGREDIENTS

1 pound sweet Italian turkey sausage, cut into 1-inch pieces

1 medium onion, diced

2 garlic cloves, sliced

1 large carrot, peeled and thinly sliced

1 celery stalk, thinly sliced

1 cup lentils

2 cups beef stock

1 can (14.5 ounces) diced tomatoes with garlic and olive oil

1 bay leaf

½ teaspoon crushed red pepper flakes (optional)

DIRECTIONS

Preheat the Flip Pan over medium-high heat for 2 minutes.

Add the sausage and brown for 3 minutes, breaking apart with a wooden spoon while doing so.

Add the onions and garlic and cook for 2 minutes longer being careful not to burn.

Add in all the remaining ingredients.

Secure the lid and set a timer for 20 minutes.

When cooking time is complete, discard the bay leaf and serve immediately.

Pizza Soup

Servings: 4

INGREDIENTS

1 pound Italian sausage, cut into 1-inch slices

3 ounces pepperoni, diced

2 tablespoons extra virgin olive oil

1 medium onion, chopped

4 garlic cloves, sliced

4 cups chicken stock

1 teaspoon salt

1 teaspoon freshly ground pepper

1 teaspoon dried oregano

1 teaspoon dried basil

1 teaspoon garlic powder

1 green bell pepper, diced

1 can (28 ounces) petite diced tomatoes

6 slices mozzarella cheese

6 oven safe bowls or crocks

DIRECTIONS

Preheat Flip Pan over medium heat.

Add the olive oil and heat for 1 minute.

Add the Italian sausage; brown well about 3 minutes.

Add the pepperonis, onions, and garlic, and cook for 2 minutes.

Add the remaining ingredients and cook over medium heat for 25 minutes.

When cooking is complete, divide the soup between oven-safe bowls.

Preheat broiler.

Top each bowl with a slice of cheese, then place the bowls under the broiler for 3 minutes or
until cheese is melted.

Serve immediately.

Delicious with crusty bread for dipping.

Poached Pears

Servings: 4

INGREDIENTS

3 cups dry, white wine

1 tablespoon cardamom pods

1 cup sugar

2 tablespoons fresh lemon juice

¼ teaspoon saffron threads

6 firm pears, peeled, stems in tact

½ teaspoon kosher salt

1 6-ounce container crème fraiche

DIRECTIONS

Add all the ingredients except the crème fraiche to the Flip Pan.

Secure the lid over medium-high heat; set a timer for 30 minutes.

When cooking is complete, using a slotted spoon transfer the pears to a platter.

With the lid open, continue to reduce cooking liquid until syrupy. About 5 minutes.

Top the pears with syrup and serve. Great served with crème fraiche.

Pork Chile Verde

Servings: 4

INGREDIENTS

2 pounds pork tenderloin, cut into 2-inch cubes
1 teaspoon sea salt
½ teaspoon fresh ground pepper
1 teaspoon ground cumin
1 teaspoon chipotle powder
1 tablespoon olive oil
2 cloves garlic, minced
1 small onion, chopped
4 wholes tomatillos, husks removed and chopped
1 tablespoon fresh lime juice
1 cup chicken stock
1 can green chili, chopped
2 tablespoons chopped fresh cilantro
sour cream, for garnish

DIRECTIONS

Preheat Flip Pan over medium heat 2 minutes.

Add the oil and increase the heat to medium-high.

Season the pork cubes with salt and pepper, then add to the Flip Pan and brown the meat on all sides, about 5 minutes.

Add the tomatillos, onions, garlic, cumin, and chipotle powder.

Cook for 2 minutes longer.

Add the lime juice, stock, and green chilies.

Secure the lid and set timer for 45 minutes.

When cook time is complete, remove lid and stir in the fresh cilantro.

Serve in bowls topped with sour cream.

Potato Leek Soup

Servings: 4

INGREDIENTS

2 tablespoons extra-virgin olive oil

2 cups leeks, sliced (white part only)

1 cup sweet onion, sliced

¼ cup diced, celery

2 cups Yukon gold potatoes, peeled and diced

½ teaspoon salt

½ teaspoon freshly ground pepper

3 cups chicken stock

1 sprig thyme

½ cup sour cream

1 teaspoon fresh chives, chopped

DIRECTIONS

Preheat the Flip Pan over medium heat for 2 minutes. Add the oil and cook 1 minute longer.

Place the leeks, onions, potatoes, and celery in the Flip Pan. Season with salt and pepper, and cook with lid open until onions are translucent, about 5 minutes.

Add the stock and thyme, secure the lid.

Set timer for 25 minutes.

When cooking time is complete, purée the soup using an immersion blender until desired consistency is achieved.

Serve topped with sour cream and chives.

Oatmeal Cookies

Servings: 6

INGREDIENTS

½ cup plus 6 tablespoons unsalted butter, softened
¾ cup packed light brown sugar
½ cup sugar
1 teaspoon vanilla extract
2 large eggs
1 teaspoon baking powder
½ teaspoon kosher salt
½ teaspoon cinnamon
1½ cups all-purpose flour
3 cups rolled oats
½ cup chocolate chips
½ cup raisins
parchment paper

DIRECTIONS

Place butter and sugars in a bowl of a stand mixer, or with a hand mixer, cream butters and sugar until light and fluffy, scraping down the sides several times in the process.

Measure your flour, baking powder, salt and cinnamon onto a sheet of parchment paper, then top with the oats.

Add eggs to butter mixture and mix in well.

Pick up sides of parchment paper to form a shoot. Slowly dump the dry ingredients into the bowl while mixing on low.

Increase speed to medium and add in the chocolate chips and raisins.

Place the parchment paper on the Flip Pan rack.

Scoop cookies onto the rack.

Place the rack in the Flip Pan, close the lid, and increase the heat to medium.

Set a timer for 15 minutes.

When timer goes off, carefully remove the parchment from the Flip Pan.

Repeat with remaining cookie dough.

Chocolate Pot de Crème

Servings: 4

INGREDIENTS

2 ounces bittersweet chocolate, finely chopped
1 cup heavy cream
1 cup whole milk
4 egg yolks
2 tablespoons sugar
½ teaspoon orange zest
⅛ teaspoon salt
1 quart water

DIRECTIONS

Apply nonstick spray to four 4-ounce ramekins; set aside.

Place the chocolate into a mixing bowl.

Pour the cream and milk into a saucepan over medium heat.

When the cream mixture begins to simmer, pour the mixture into the bowl with the chocolate; stir until smooth.

In a separate bowl, combine remaining ingredients, except water.

Slowly pour the chocolate mixture into the yolk mixture; mix well.

Divide the mixture between the ramekins.

Wrap each ramekin in aluminum foil.

Pour the water into the Flip Pan.

Place the rack in the Flip Pan and bring the water to a boil over medium high heat.

Once the water comes to a boil, place the ramekins in the Jumbo Flip Pan; secure lid.

Set timer for 12 minutes.

When cooking is complete, remove the ramekins and let rest at room temperature for 30 minutes.

Remove the foil and serve with a dab of whipped cream.

Red Lager Corned Beef and Cabbage

Servings: 4

INGREDIENTS

12 ounces red lager like Killian's or bass ale

2 cups beef stock

1½ pounds corned beef brisket

4 cloves garlic

1 tablespoon pickling spice

1 large sweet onion, quartered

4 large carrots, peeled and cut into 2-inch pieces

2 stalks celery, cut into 2-inch pieces

1 small head of cabbage, cut into quarters

4 red bliss potatoes

DIRECTIONS

Place the lager, stock, corned beef, garlic, pickling spice, and onion in the Flip Pan.

Secure the lid, and bring to a rapid boil over medium-high heat, about 10 minutes.

Once the Flip Pan comes to a boil, lower heat to medium and cook for 90 minutes.

Once cook time is complete, open the lid and add remaining ingredients.

Set timer for 20 minutes.

Remove ingredients to a platter and serve with spicy mustard and cider vinegar on the side.

Spicy Sausage Rice

Servings: 6

INGREDIENTS

1 tablespoon extra-virgin olive oil

1 medium onion, diced

1 pound andouille smoked sausage, thinly sliced

1 red bell pepper, diced

3 garlic cloves, minced

2 tablespoons tomato paste

1 teaspoon salt

½ teaspoon cayenne pepper

1 teaspoon cumin

1 tablespoon Hungarian paprika

½ teaspoon black pepper

½ teaspoon marjoram

2 cups long-grain rice, rinsed

4 cups beef stock

DIRECTIONS

Preheat Flip Pan over medium heat for 2 minutes. Add oil and cook for 1 minute longer.

Add the onions to the Flip Pan and cook for 2 minutes, stirring occasionally; add the sausage and cook for 2 minutes longer.

Add the red pepper and garlic to the Flip Pan; stir.

Add the tomato paste to the Flip Pan and cook for an additional 2 minutes.

Add remaining ingredients to the Flip Pan.

Secure lid and set timer for 20 minutes.

When cooking is complete, stir and serve immediately.

Stuffed Peppers

Servings: 4

INGREDIENTS

1 pound lean ground beef

1 teaspoon salt

1 teaspoon freshly ground pepper

1 medium sweet onion, chopped

3 garlic cloves, minced

4 threads saffron

1 can (14.5 ounces) petite diced tomatoes

½ cup couscous, grande size

1 cup chicken stock

¼ cup Parmesan cheese, grated

4 large bell peppers

1 cup water

1 cup tomato sauce

DIRECTIONS

Preheat Flip Pan over medium high heat for 2 minutes.

Add the ground beef and cook meat while breaking it apart with a wooden spoon.

After 4 minutes, add the salt and pepper and onions and cook for 2 minutes longer.

Add the saffron and garlic and cook 1 minute longer.

Add the canned tomatoes and couscous and stock to Flip Pan, stir.

Secure the Flip Pan lid and set timer for 10 minutes.

When cook time is complete, pour ingredients into a large bowl, stir in cheese, and let cool.

Remove the tops and membranes from the bell peppers; set aside the tops.

Divide the meat mixture evenly between the peppers.

Rinse the Flip Pan, add the water and rack.

Place the peppers on the rack, top each pepper with tomato sauce.

Place the Flip Pan on medium high heat, secure lid, and set timer for 15 minutes.

When cooking is complete, serve immediately with additional sauce if you wish.

Barbecue Chicken

Servings: 4

INGREDIENTS

1 whole fryer, cut into 8 pieces
1 tablespoon olive oil
1 teaspoon salt
1 teaspoon freshly ground pepper
1 teaspoon dry mustard
1 teaspoon paprika
1 medium onion, diced
3 garlic cloves, minced
½ cup chicken stock
2 tablespoons cider vinegar
¼ cup brown sugar
¼ cup ketchup
¼ cup molasses

DIRECTIONS

Preheat the Jumbo Flip Pan over medium heat.

Rub chicken parts with oil and season with salt and pepper.

Place chicken parts into the Flip Pan, skin side down, and increase heat to medium-high.

Brown chicken parts for 4 minutes until skin is golden brown; using tongs turn the chicken.

Cook for an additional 4 minutes with lid open.

Turn chicken parts again and add in remaining ingredients, stir and scrape up the browned bits on bottom of the pan.

Secure Flip Pan lid, lower heat to medium.

Cook for 30 minutes.

Chicken Curry in a Hurry

Servings: 4

INGREDIENTS

2 pounds skinless chicken legs

1 tablespoon olive oil

½ cup chicken stock

1 cup diced tomato

¼ cup brown sugar

1 tablespoon curry powder

1 teaspoon garam masala

1 medium onion, chopped

1 red bell pepper, julienned

1 cup yogurt, strained to remove excess water

1 tablespoon fresh cilantro leaves, chopped

DIRECTIONS

Preheat Jumbo Flip Pan over medium heat.

Rub the chicken legs with oil, add the legs to the Flip Pan and brown on all sides, about 8 minutes.

Add the remaining ingredients except for yogurt and cilantro.

Stir and scrape up the browned bits off the bottom of the pan.

Secure lid and set timer for 20 minutes.

When cooking is complete, transfer the chicken legs to a platter.

With the lid open, allow the sauce to reduce in the Flip Pan until it is thick and syrupy. Stir in the yogurt.

Pour mixture over the chicken legs, top with cilantro and serve.

Triple Flip Pan

Italian Sausage with Fennel and Peppers

Servings: 2

INGREDIENTS

1 pound sweet Italian sausage
1 sweet onion, sliced
1 cup fennel bulb, sliced
1 red bell pepper, julienned
1 green bell pepper, julienned
1 tablespoon olive oil

DIRECTIONS

Preheat Flip Pan, top and bottom, on medium heat for 2–3 minutes per side.

Place sausage in Flip Pan and close lid.

Cook for 4 minutes per side.

Remove sausage and cut lengthwise.

In a bowl, toss the onion, fennel and peppers in olive oil.

Place sausage and vegetables in Flip Pan; close lid.

Cook 4 minutes per side and serve.

Blueberry Pancakes

Servings: 4

1¾ cups all-purpose flour

2 tablespoons sugar

1 teaspoon baking powder

½ teaspoon baking soda

½ teaspoon salt

2 large eggs

1 cup milk, more if needed

1 cup sour cream

¼ cup butter, melted

½ teaspoon vanilla extract

1½ cups fresh or frozen blueberries

½ teaspoon lemon zest

nonstick cooking spray

DIRECTIONS

Sift the flour, sugar, baking powder, baking soda, and salt into a large mixing bowl.

In a separate bowl, lightly whisk eggs.

Add the milk, sour cream, half the melted butter and the vanilla extract, whisking to blend.

Make a well in the dry ingredients and pour the egg mixture into it.

Whisk the ingredients together, just until blended.

Fold the blueberries and lemon zest into the batter.

Apply nonstick to triple Flip Pan.

Preheat triple Flip Pan over medium heat, 2–3 minutes per side.

Fill each cup halfway with batter; close lid.

Cook for 2 minutes per side.

Serve immediately.

Berry-Good Rhubarb Crisp

Servings: 8

5 cups rhubarb, chopped, fresh or frozen

3 cups strawberries, sliced, fresh or frozen

¾ cup sugar

2 teaspoons quick cook tapioca

5 tablespoons unsalted butter

½ cup light brown sugar

¼ cup all-purpose flour

½ cup rolled oats

½ teaspoon apple pie spice

½ cup walnuts

nonstick cooking spray

DIRECTIONS

In a bowl, combine rhubarb, strawberries, sugar, and tapioca.

In a food processor, combine butter, brown sugar, flour, oats, apple pie spice, and walnuts.

Pulse 4 times. Avoid overmixing.

Apply nonstick to Flip Pan.

Preheat triple Flip Pan over medium heat for 2–3 minutes per side.

Put ingredients from processor in Flip Pan and toast for 1–2 minutes.

Add the fruit mixture and flip.

Cook for 5 minutes; serve with ice cream.

Thai Scallop Kabobs

Servings: 4

INGREDIENTS

16 jumbo sea scallops
16 snap peas
1 red bell pepper, cut into 1-inch pieces
½ cup Thai marinade

DIRECTIONS

Assemble six skewers by alternating scallops, snap peas, and red peppers.

In a bowl, combine kabobs and with the marinade; let marinate for 30 minutes.

Preheat Flip Pan, top and bottom, on medium heat for 2–3 minutes per side.

Place kabobs in Flip Pan and close lid

Cook for 3 minutes per side and serve.

Breakfast Sandwiches

Servings: 2

INGREDIENTS

4 slices brioche bread, or 2 English muffins

nonstick spray

¼ pound ground sausage, turkey or pork, formed into round patties

3 large eggs, beaten

2 slices cheddar cheese

2 slices ripe tomatoes

DIRECTIONS

Preheat Triple Flip Pan over medium heat for 3 minutes per side.

If using bread, cut it to the size of the rings.

Spray the Triple Flip with nonstick spray.

With ring side down, add the bread to the rings and toast for 2 minutes per side.

Remove the bread, add the sausage patties, and cook with lid closed for 3 minutes.

Divide the beaten eggs between the two remaining rings.

Close Flip Pan and cook for 2 minutes, shaking occasionally.

Flip and open to add the cheese slices to the top of each sausage.

Close Flip Pan and continue to cook for 3 minutes longer.

To assemble sandwich, on one slice of bread place sausage, then egg, then tomato slice, then top with remaining slice of bread; repeat with the remaining ingredients.

Addie Anderson's Toad in the Hole

Servings: 1–2

Addie is the daughter of the designer of this incredible pan. She suffers from terrible food allergies, and Curtis wanted to make this a pan that she could easily cook with, since dining out can be so risky. Addie appeared on TV with me preparing her breakfast specialty. She is too cute!!!

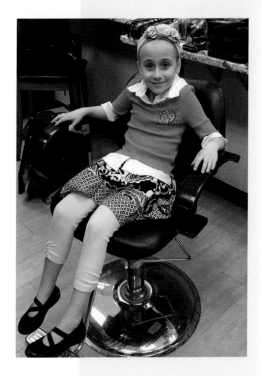

INGREDIENTS

1 slice gluten-free or white bread

1 teaspoon extra-virgin olive oil or nonstick spray

1 large egg

pinch of salt

pinch of freshly ground pepper

DIRECTIONS

Cut a 1½-inch hole in the center of bread slice using a cookie cutter or a small juice glass.

Apply olive oil or nonstick spray to Flip Pan.

Preheat Flip Pan, top and bottom, on medium heat for 2–3 minutes per side.

Place bread slice on griddle side of Flip Pan and crack an egg into the center of the hole; season with salt and pepper; close lid.

Cook for 2–3 minutes per side. Depending on how runny you want your yolk.

Pesto Grilled Shrimp

Servings: 2

INGREDIENTS

4 cups baby spinach leaves

1 teaspoon lemon juice

½ teaspoon salt

½ teaspoon freshly ground pepper

nonstick cooking spray

1 pound jumbo shrimp, peeled and deveined

½ cup My Favorite Pesto, page 166, or store bought

DIRECTIONS

In a bowl, combine spinach, lemon juice, salt and pepper; mix.

Preheat Flip Pan, top and bottom, on medium heat for 2–3 minutes per side.

Apply nonstick spray to Flip Pan.

Place spinach mixture in Flip Pan; close lid.

Cook for 1 minute per side, and then transfer to a plate.

In a separate bowl, combine shrimp and pesto.

Reapply nonstick to Flip Pan.

Place shrimp in Flip Pan; close lid.

Grill for 4 minutes per side.

Place shrimp on spinach and serve.

Green Bean Casserole

Servings: 6

INGREDIENTS

2 pounds green beans, washed and stems removed

1 medium sweet onion, thinly sliced

1 tablespoon extra-virgin olive oil

1 cup mushrooms, sliced

½ tablespoon salted butter

½ teaspoon freshly ground pepper

1 teaspoon kosher salt

1 tablespoon sherry

1 can (10¾ ounces) cream of mushroom soup

1 cup French fried onions

DIRECTIONS

Preheat Flip Pan over medium heat, 2–3 minutes per side.

Place all ingredients except mushroom soup and French fried onions in Flip Pan; close lid.

Cook for 5 minutes, open lid, add mushroom soup and stir; close lid.

Cook for 1 additional minute, top with fried onions, and serve.

Low-Fat Strada

Servings: 6

INGREDIENTS

6 cups whole-grain bread, cubed

1 cup reduced-fat mozzarella or cheddar cheese, shredded

1 pound bulk turkey breakfast sausage, cooked and crumbled

½ cup onion, diced

1 cup broccoli florets

2 cups egg substitute

3 cups low-fat milk

1 teaspoon salt

½ teaspoon dry mustard

nonstick cooking spray

½ cup Parmesan cheese, grated

DIRECTIONS

In a bowl, combine all ingredients except Parmesan cheese.

Apply nonstick to Flip Pan.

Preheat Flip Pan over medium heat for 2–3 minutes per side.

Place mixed ingredients into Flip Pan, close lid.

Cook for 4 minutes, open and add Parmesan cheese. Flip and cook for an additional 4 minutes.

Serve immediately.

Maple Squash Rings

Servings: 2

INGREDIENTS

2 tablespoons butter, softened

4 slices acorn squash, seeds removed and cut 2 inches thick

2 tablespoons brown sugar

2 teaspoons maple syrup

1 teaspoon lemon juice

½ teaspoon sea salt

nonstick spray

3 teaspoons water

DIRECTIONS

Preheat Flip Pan, top and bottom, on medium heat for 2–3 minutes per side.

Add the butter to the Flip Pan and melt (1 minute)

Place the squash rings in the Flip Pan, sprinkle with brown sugar, syrup, lemon juice and salt.

Spray the top of the Flip Pan with nonstick spray.

Close the Flip Pan and cook for 5 minutes.

Flip and cook for 5 minutes longer.

Add a couple teaspoons of water, flip and cook 5 minutes longer. Cook until tender.

Nick Torre's Juicy Lucy

Servings: 4

My darling Nick Torre is fascinated with cooking and food. I give him private cooking lessons because he is so curious. This is his version of the Minnesota classic Juicy Lucy burger.

INGREDIENTS

2 pounds ground chuck
½ cup cheddar cheese, shredded
8 pickle slices
nonstick cooking spray
¼ teaspoon salt
¼ teaspoon pepper

DIRECTIONS

Separate ground chuck into 8 balls, and place on a cutting board, pressing into patties.

Make a well in each patty, pressing down the middle with your fingers.

Fill each well with cheese, then with pickle slices; cover with a remaining patty.

Pinch sides of the patties to seal.

Apply nonstick spray to Flip Pan.

Preheat Flip Pan over medium heat for 2–3 minutes per side.

Place burgers in the Triple Flip rings, season with salt and pepper; close lid.

Cook for 4 minutes per side over medium heat.

Serve with your favorite toppings.

Michelle Kubala Piro's Chicken Cordon Bleu

Servings: 4

INGREDIENTS

4 chicken breasts, skinless and boneless
½ teaspoon salt
½ teaspoon freshly ground pepper
4 ham slices
4 Swiss cheese slices
¼ cup Parmesan cheese
½ cup flour
½ cup Italian bread crumbs
½ cup milk
1 egg, beaten
nonstick cooking spray
½ cup white wine
½ teaspoon corn starch
½ cup chicken broth

DIRECTIONS

Season chicken breast with salt and pepper and place on cutting board. Pound to flatten.

Lay 1 piece of ham and 1 piece of cheese on each chicken breast; folding the sides of the ham over the cheese. Fold over chicken and secure with toothpicks.

In a bowl, combine Parmesan cheese, flour and Italian bread crumbs.

In another bowl combine milk and egg, mix well.

Apply nonstick to Flip Pan and preheat over medium heat 2–3 minutes per side.

Dip each chicken breast into egg mixture, then into breadcrumbs.

Place chicken breasts into Flip Pan; close lid.

Cook for 10 minutes, flip and cook for another 10 minutes, depending on size.

Transfer chicken to a platter, cover loosely.

Add wine to Flip Pan to deglaze.

Mix corn starch with stock, add to the wine, close lid and simmer until thickened.

Pour gravy over chicken and serve.

Mini Mediterranean Frittatas

Servings: 4

INGREDIENTS

nonstick cooking spray

½ cup onion, diced

4 medium mushrooms, chopped

1 clove garlic, minced

¼ tablespoon salt

pinch of dried red pepper flakes

4 eggs

2 cups baby spinach

1 tablespoon cream

2 tablespoons goat cheese

DIRECTIONS

Apply nonstick spray to Flip Pan.

Preheat Flip Pan over medium heat for 2–3 minutes per side.

Add onion, mushrooms, garlic, salt, spinach and red pepper flakes, divided evenly, to each cup; close lid.

Cook for 1 minute, shaking a few times.

In another bowl, whisk together the spinach, cream and goat cheese.

Divide the egg mixture between the four cups; close lid.

Cook for 1 minute, open lid and place equal parts of goat cheese on each frittata; close lid.

Flip Pan and cook for additional 1 minute, or until cheese is melted.

Serve immediately.

Stuffed Cabbage Rolls

Servings: 6

INGREDIENTS

1 large head of cabbage

1 pound extra-lean ground beef

½ cup onion, minced

1 teaspoon salt

1 teaspoon ground pepper

1 large egg, beaten

1 tablespoon Worcestershire sauce

1 cup rice, cooked

1 can (8 ounces) tomato sauce

1 tablespoon sugar

1 teaspoon beef stock

2 cups mozzarella cheese, shredded

DIRECTIONS

Separate cabbage into 12 large leaves.

Boil or steam cabbage until flexible, but not mushy. Drain and cool.

In a bowl, combine beef, onion, salt, pepper, egg and Worcestershire sauce.

Add rice to bowl; mix well

Place ¼ cup of beef mixture in the center of each cabbage leaf.

Fold in sides and roll ends over meat.

Preheat Flip Pan over medium heat for 2–3 minutes per side.

In a bowl, combine tomato sauce, sugar and beef stock, and pour into Flip Pan; close lid.

Cook 1 minute, open and place cabbage rolls into Flip Pan; close lid.

Cook for additional 10 minutes.

Add mozzarella; close lid and cook for 1 additional minute.

Serve immediately.

Rhubarb Berry Crisp

Servings: 8

INGREDIENTS

5 cups rhubarb, chopped, fresh or frozen

3 cups strawberries, sliced, fresh or frozen

¾ cup sugar

2 teaspoons quick cook tapioca

5 tablespoons unsalted butter

½ cup light brown sugar

¼ cup all-purpose flour

½ cup rolled oats

½ teaspoon apple pie spice

½ cup walnuts

nonstick cooking spray

DIRECTIONS

In a bowl, combine rhubarb, strawberries, sugar and tapioca.

In a food processor, combine butter, brown sugar, flour, oats, apple pie spice and walnuts.

Pulse 4 times. Avoid overmixing.

Apply nonstick to Flip Pan.

Preheat Triple Flip Pan over medium heat for 2–3 minutes per side.

Place ingredients from processor into Flip Pan and toast for 1–2 minutes.

Add the fruit mixture, and flip.

Cook for 5 minutes; serve with ice cream.

Shepherd's Pie

Servings: 4

INGREDIENTS

1 cup water

2 pounds potatoes, such as russets, peeled and cubed

2 tablespoons sour cream, or softened cream cheese

1 large egg yolk

½ cup cream, vegetable stock, or chicken stock

1 tablespoon extra-virgin olive oil

1¾ pound ground beef or lamb

¼ teaspoon salt

¼ teaspoon freshly ground pepper

1 carrot, peeled and chopped

1 onion, chopped

2 tablespoons butter

2 tablespoons all-purpose flour

1 cup beef stock

2 teaspoons Worcestershire sauce

½ cup frozen peas

¼ cup cheddar cheese, shredded

Preheat Flip Pan over medium heat for 2–3 minutes per side.

Add water to Flip Pan, add potatoes and a pinch of salt; close lid.

Cook for 10 minutes, or until tender.

Drain potatoes and pour into a bowl.

In a separate bowl, combine sour cream or cream cheese, egg yolk, and cream or stock; mix well.

Pour cream mixture onto potatoes and mash until smooth; set aside.

Add oil to Flip Pan and let heat over medium heat for 1–2 minutes; add beef or lamb.

Season with salt and pepper; close lid.

Cook for 2–3 minutes, drain off excess drippings. Add carrots and onions to the meat; close lid.

Cook an additional 5 minutes.

In a small skillet, cook butter and flour together over medium heat.

Whisk in stock and Worcestershire sauce, let thicken for 1 minute.

Add gravy to meat and vegetables; stir in peas.

Spoon potatoes evenly over the meat, sprinkle with shredded cheddar; close lid.

Cook for 2–3 minutes until heated through, and cheese is melted.

Remove from pan and let sit for 2 minutes before cutting.

S'mores

Servings: 4

INGREDIENTS

1 frozen family-sized pound cake, cut into ½-inch slices
2 tablespoons butter, room temperature
4 thin dark chocolate bars, cut into even pieces
12 large marshmallows, sliced lengthwise
powdered sugar

DIRECTIONS

Preheat Flip Pan, top and bottom, on medium heat for 2–3 minutes per side.

Spread butter on one side of 2 slices of pound cake and place them butter-side down on a cutting board.

Top one cake slice with chocolate and marshmallows; cover with other cake slice, butter-side up.

Repeat step with remaining ingredients, except powdered sugar.

Place s'mores into Flip Pan; close lid.

Cook for 2 minutes per side.

Dust s'mores with powdered sugar and serve.

Pork Chops L'Orange

Servings: 4

INGREDIENTS

4 pork chops, 2 inches thick, bone-in

1 tablespoon extra-virgin olive oil, divided

½ teaspoon salt

½ teaspoon fresh ground pepper

½ cup chicken stock

¼ cup brown sugar

1 teaspoon cider vinegar

1 teaspoon freshly grated ginger

1 tablespoon soy sauce

1 teaspoon orange zest

1 sprig fresh thyme

½ teaspoon black pepper

2 oranges, peeled and sectioned, or ½ cup drained mandarin oranges

DIRECTIONS

Rub the pork chops with olive oil, then season with salt and pepper.

Preheat Flip Pan over medium heat for 2 minutes.

Add the oil and heat for 1 minute longer then increase the heat to medium-high. Place the pork chops into the Flip Pan and brown for 3 minutes per side.

Add the chicken stock and remaining ingredients to the Flip Pan; secure lid.

Lower heat to medium and set timer for 30 minutes.

Spoon the sauce over pork chops; serve immediately.

Swiss Steak

Servings: 6

2 pounds beef round steak, cut into ¾-inch cubes

1 teaspoon steak seasoning

1 tablespoon extra-virgin olive oil

1 large sweet onion, thinly sliced

1 can (14½ ounces) diced tomatoes with juice, basil and garlic

½ cup celery, chopped

½ cup carrot, sliced

1 jar (12 ounces) beef gravy

cooked noodles

DIRECTIONS

Preheat Flip Pan over medium heat for 2–3 minutes per side.

Rub beef with steak seasoning.

Add oil to Flip Pan, add meat and brown 2–3 minutes. Flip pan, add onions, and cook for additional 2–3 minutes.

Add remaining ingredients, except noodles; close lid.

Cook for 10 minutes per side.

Serve over noodles.

Stuffed French Toast

Servings: 4

INGREDIENTS

4 large eggs

¼ cup cream

1 teaspoon vanilla

2 tablespoons sugar

1 cup strawberries or raspberries, fresh or frozen

½ cup raspberry preserves

2 tablespoons raspberry flavored liqueur

1 package (4 ounces) berry-flavored cream cheese

8 slices of bread

nonstick cooking spray

½ cup cornflakes

½ cup almonds, slivered

¼ cup butter

1 tablespoon powdered sugar

DIRECTIONS

In a shallow baking dish mix eggs, cream, vanilla and sugar.

In a separate bowl, blend berries, preserves, liqueur and cream cheese.

One at a time, dip 4 slices of bread into the egg mixture, then top each with berry mixture. Remove to a platter.

Dip remaining slices of bread in remaining egg mixture, placing each slice on top of the others to form four sandwiches.

Apply nonstick to Flip Pan and heat over medium heat, 2–3 minutes per side.

Place cornflakes and almonds on a plate, press each sandwich in the cornflakes coating both sides.

Place each sandwich on the griddle side.

Cook for 4 minutes, then flip and cook for additional 3 minutes or until golden brown and cooked through.

Serve immediately with butter and dusted with powder sugar.

Tamale Pie

Servings: 6

INGREDIENTS

1 package (16 ounces) corn bread mix

nonstick cooking spray

2 pounds lean ground beef, cooked and drained

1 cup onion, diced

1 package chili seasoning

2 cans (28 ounces) tomatoes with green peppers

1 can (14 ounces) whole kernel corn, drained

1 can (2 ¼ ounces) sliced ripe olives, drained

1 cup cheddar cheese, shredded

DIRECTIONS

Prepare corn bread mix according to box instructions.

Apply nonstick spray to Flip Pan.

Preheat Flip Pan over medium heat for 2–3 minutes per side.

Add all ingredients, except corn bread batter and cheddar cheese, stir well; close lid.

Cook for 5 minutes; open lid and pour batter over meat and vegetables.

Cook for 5 minutes; open lid, sprinkle cheddar evenly over cornbread.

Cook for an additional minute.

Serve immediately.

Marinades and Sauces

Balsamic Marinade

Servings: 6

INGREDIENTS

⅓ cup balsamic vinegar

2 cloves garlic

½ teaspoon sea salt

½ teaspoon freshly ground pepper

⅔ cup extra-virgin olive oil
or grapeseed oil

DIRECTIONS

Place all the ingredients except the oil
in a blender.

Blend the ingredients well, slowly
drizzle oil through the lid cap with
motor running, process until well
combined.

Greek Dressing or Marinade

Yields 1 cup

INGREDIENTS

4 tablespoons fresh lemon juice

1 teaspoon garlic powder

1 teaspoon sea salt

2 teaspoons freshly ground pepper

2 teaspoons oregano

6 fresh mint leaves

1 cup extra-virgin olive oil

DIRECTIONS

In a food processor or blender, combine
all ingredients, except oil.

While processing, slowly drizzle in oil.

Mojo Marinade

Yields 1½ cups

INGREDIENTS

½ cup sour orange juice

4 garlic cloves

2 teaspoons ground cumin

½ teaspoon sea salt

½ teaspoon fresh ground pepper

¼ cup cilantro

1 cup extra virgin olive oil

DIRECTIONS

Place all ingredients, except oil, into a food processor or blender.

While processing, slowly drizzle in oil.

Mango Salsa

Yields 1½ cups

INGREDIENTS

1 cup mango, diced

¼ cup red onion, minced

½ cup bell pepper, diced

1 jalapeno, seeded and membrane removed

1 tablespoon cilantro, chopped

1 teaspoon fresh lime juice

DIRECTIONS

In a bowl, combine all ingredients.

Deb's Pico de Gallo

Servings: 4

INGREDIENTS

1 pint grape tomatoes

1 tomatillo, peeled

1 serrano chili, seeds removed

2 garlic cloves

3 green onions

1 small bell pepper

½ (10-ounce) can tomatoes with green chili

¼ cup fresh cilantro

1 teaspoon sea salt

½ teaspoon freshly ground pepper

3 tablespoons fresh lime juice

2 teaspoons extra-virgin olive oil

DIRECTIONS

Place all ingredients into a food processor.

Pulse until desired consistency.

Barbecue Sauce

Yields 1 cup

INGREDIENTS

½ cup ketchup
½ cup brown sugar
1 tablespoon cider vinegar
1 tablespoon molasses
1 teaspoon mustard
¼ cup bourbon
1 teaspoon sea salt

DIRECTIONS

Place all ingredients into a saucepan;
bring to a simmer.

Simmer for 15 minutes.

Barbecue Rub

Yields ¼ cup

INGREDIENTS

1 tablespoon kosher salt
1 teaspoon garlic powder
1 teaspoon onion powder
1 teaspoon chipotle powder
1 teaspoon smoked paprika
1 tablespoon brown sugar
½ teaspoon ground cumin
½ teaspoon ground coriander
1 teaspoon freshly ground pepper

DIRECTIONS

Combine all ingredients.

Store in an airtight container.

Buffalo Wing Sauce

Yields ½ cup

INGREDIENTS

½ cup unsalted butter, melted
⅔ cup Louisiana hot sauce
1½ teaspoons cider vinegar
1 teaspoon soy sauce
1 tablespoon ketchup

DIRECTIONS

In a bowl, combine all ingredients;
mix well.

Jerk Rub

Yields ¼ cup

INGREDIENTS

1 tablespoon sea salt
1 tablespoon cayenne pepper
1 teaspoon smoked paprika
1 teaspoon cinnamon
1 teaspoon nutmeg
1 teaspoon ground allspice
1 teaspoon onion powder
2 teaspoons thyme
1 teaspoon ground ginger

DIRECTIONS

In a bowl, combine all ingredients.

Store in an airtight container.

My Favorite Pesto

Servings: 8

INGREDIENTS

- 2 garlic cloves
- 3 tablespoons butter
- ½ teaspoon freshly ground pepper
- ½ cup Parmigiano-Reggiano cheese, grated
- 3 cups fresh basil leaves
- 1 cup baby spinach leaves
- ½ cup extra-virgin olive oil

DIRECTIONS

In a food processor or blender, combine all ingredients, except oil.

While processing, slowly drizzle oil into processor.

Marinara Sauce

Servings: 8

INGREDIENTS

- ¼ cup extra-virgin olive oil
- 1 medium onion, minced
- 2 garlic cloves, minced
- 3 tablespoons tomato paste
- 1 can (28 ounces) crushed tomatoes
- 1 teaspoon sea salt
- ½ teaspoon freshly ground pepper
- 1 tablespoon fresh basil, chopped
- ½ teaspoon oregano
- 1 tablespoon flat leaf parsley, chopped

DIRECTIONS

Preheat Jumbo Flip Pan over medium heat, uncovered.

Add the oil and let heat for 2 minutes.

Add onions and garlic to the pan; sauté for 2 minutes.

Add tomato paste to pan and cook for 3 minutes.

Add remaining ingredients, close lid, and cook for 15 minutes.

Delicious over pasta.

Recipe Index